OUT OF NOWHERE

The Detroit Tigers' Magical 2006 Season

TRIUMPH
BOOKS

Ivan Rodriguez provided steady leadership on both offense and defense for the Tigers throughout the 2006 season.

Published by Triumph Books, Chicago.

TEXT BY
GEORGE CANTOR

COPY EDITOR
RICHARD BENJAMIN

PHOTOGRAPHY BY
AP/WIDE WORLD PHOTOS

Content packaged by Mojo Media, Inc.
Editor: Joe Funk
Creative Director: Jason Hinman

This book is available in quantity at special discounts for your group or organization.
For further information, contact:

Triumph Books
542 South Dearborn Street
Suite 750
Chicago, IL 60605

Chicago, Illinois 60605
Phone: (312) 939-3330
Fax: (312) 663-3557

Printed in the United States of America

The Detroit Tigers' Magical 2006 Season

Contents

A Baseball Town Reborn

At Long Last, Fun at the Old Ballpark

This is how a stadium becomes a ballpark:

With lines stretching back to the street from every ticket window.

With crowds staying through the ninth inning because it is possible, maybe even likely, that the Tigers will find a way to pull it out.

With chants of "Let's Go, Tigers" coming from every corner of the sold-out stands.

With little kids wearing caps with the Old English D in front, instead of the insignia of the Yankees or Red Sox.

With gasps of disbelief when the scoreboard registers 102 miles an hour as the speed of a Joel Zumaya fastball.

With shouts of exhilaration as Craig Monroe drives in another run in the clutch.

With crowds lingering for hours before and after the game at the bars and restaurants right across Woodward Avenue.

With a feeling of joyful anticipation as the customers walk through the turnstiles, and a sense that they may well see something absolutely remarkable today.

For the previous six years of its brief history, Comerica Park was a beautiful stadium. Its views of the downtown Detroit skyline were fine. Its displays of Tigers history and statues of great players in the centerfield concourse were inspiring. The massive scoreboard, the fountain, the ample concession stands—all of it very nice.

But it wasn't a ballpark. Because a ballpark is a place filled with memories. Last-ditch rallies and brilliant pitching and gravity-defying catches. Memories of games pulled out and pennants won, shared with those who are closest to you.

There had been none of that at Comerica Park. From its opening in April 2000 up to the start of the 2006 season, the Tigers were the worst team in baseball. They were 199 games under .500 and used up managers like wet towels. They came within a game in 2003 of posting the worst record of any team in any season of modern baseball history. They had not finished with a winning record in 16 seasons.

One year, their sole representative on the American League All Star team was Robert Fick. Robert Fick!

Players were shuffled in and out of town in seemingly random patterns. Old heroes from the 1984 World Champions were brought in to manage, coach and try to right the sinking ship. Coverage of the team slipped deeper and deeper into the sports pages of the daily newspapers.

Attendance figures fell all the way back to the low ebb of Tiger Stadium's final years. The boost a new

The Detroit Tigers' Magical 2006 Season

Tiger Stadium is shown near downtown Detroit in this July 16, 2003, file photo. In Comerica Park the Motor City's skyline looms over the outfield where Ty Cobb and Al Kaline are honored. Comerica Park is what Tiger Stadium wasn't, and that is both good and bad.

The front entrance to Comerica Park, a decidedly different experience than the old Tiger Stadium.

hot summer afternoons. Why couldn't it have been built more along the lines of good old Tiger Stadium, with a sense of nostalgic intimacy?

It was the stadium nobody loved. But in a matter of weeks in the spring of 2006, it was all forgotten.

From out of nowhere, the sad sack Tigers, once among the proudest franchises in baseball, had been restored to respect. Excitement rippled through every corner of the state, every place in America inhabited by their far-flung fans. Comerica Park had suddenly become a house of dreams, a ballpark, at last.

It was the sheer improbability of it all that was so stunning. Usually there is a slow buildup, a few bumps and bruises along the way, some psychological preparation for the big breakthrough. That's how it had been with the 1968 and 1984 World Series winners. That's the way it had gone with recent Red Wings and Pistons championship seasons, too.

There had been nothing like this; a team shooting like a rocket out of the dark cellar of failure and into the stars.

stadium was supposed to give the franchise and the city had been squandered.

Carping about Comerica was constant. The field boxes were pitched too low so the view of those sitting closest to the field was obstructed. The field's dimensions were way too big so free-agent power hitters would never come here. Most seats had no shade on

If you had been watching closely, though, it may have been foreseeable as early as November 2001. That's when the team hired David Dombrowski and named him president.

He holds the record for building an expansion franchise into a World Series winner. It took him just five years to do that with the Florida Marlins. The team he took over in Detroit may have been a little worse than those original Marlins.

With the exception of Brandon Inge, not a single

The hiring of Dave Dombrowski as team president in 2001 marked a key turning point in the fortunes of the Detroit Tigers.

Dave Dombrowski poses with first-round draft pick, second overall, Justin Verlander in November, 2004.

player who was with the ballclub when he arrived is still there. Like the grown-up called in to restore order to a slaphappy frat house, Dombrowski cleaned it out.

"I think you have to be careful when you talk about that," he says. "Because you're talking about peoples' lives. You don't ever want to downplay that.

"The most important thing is having good people in your organization. That's your foundation for success. In the places I had been before--Montreal and Florida--it was a whole new group. Coming to Detroit was a little different. A lot of people were on board who were given the opportunity to stay, and that's worked out well."

Nonetheless, the Tigers had a well-deserved reputation for making terrible draft selections and pointless trades. After the first six games of the 2002 season--

all losses--he had fired the manager and general manager and named himself to the latter position.

Dombrowski is blessed with a phenomenal memory and can reel off the career statistics of players throughout organized baseball. He was smart enough to know the situation was going to get a whole lot worse before it could begin to get better. The already shaky fan base was not going to like the total reconstruction project he had in mind for 2003. So he brought in Alan Trammell to buy some time and take one for the franchise.

An authentic Detroit hero, Trammell had no managerial experience. To make matters worse, he brought in similarly inexperienced teammates from '84, Kirk Gibson and Lance Parrish, as his coaches.

The results were as sad as they were inevitable. The 119-loss first season was stunning. But Detroit was willing to give Tram some slack.

Despite some modest improvement on the field and at the gate by 2005--it couldn't very well get much worse--Trammell had used up his portion of good will.

A team that many thought would contend for the division title, or at least finish at .500, came in 10 games under the break-even point. Sure, there were injuries. But the Tigers still seemed woefully undermanned and poorly run when compared to Chicago, Cleveland and Minnesota--the three best teams in the division. The fans turned against Trammell. By late July, he had lost control of the clubhouse, too.

One month shy of his fourth anniversary with the club, Dombrowski made his most important decision yet. When he did, he put an old dream back on track. ∎

A smiling Dave Dombrowski helps newly hired manager Jim Leyland into a Detroit Tigers jersey in October, 2005.

Meet the New Boss
Leyland's Intensity Gives Franchise a New Face

By his own admission, Jim Leyland had been a burnt-out case. He walked out of the managerial job in Colorado in 1999 after just one season. It had been a 90-loss year and "after 35 years in the dugout, I've had enough," he said.

Leyland was then almost 55 and looked a lot older than that. He wanted more time with his young family back in Pittsburgh. He had won his Championship ring with the 1997 Marlins. There was nothing left to prove.

It was to this man that Dombrowski turned in October 2005 to lead the Tigers.

Leyland insisted he didn't know a thing about the roster of his new team. But he'd had a bad taste in his mouth for six years and he needed to get it out. And it wasn't from the cigarettes he was always puffing, either.

"I did a lousy job my last year of managing," he said. "I stunk, and when I left there I sincerely believed that I would not manage again. But I missed the competition and I did not want my managerial career to end [that way]. This stuck in my craw a little bit."

Dombrowski praised him as a manager in the mold of Tony LaRussa and Bobby Cox. That was understandable. After all, this was the guy who had won it all for him with the Marlins. "The passion is back within him," he said.

Left unspoken was the fact that this was the restoration of a dream deferred. Leyland had grown up in the Detroit organization. Signed as one of the top athletes in the Toledo area, he never had the sort of talent as a catcher that would take him to the majors. Especially with Bill Freehan in the way with the big club.

But he had a great baseball mind, and it was understood while Leyland was still in his late 20s that he was being groomed for the Detroit job. He became the man who prepared the franchise's rising stars for the big leagues.

Kirk Gibson recalls that Leyland met him at the Tampa airport when he reported to his first Class A assignment in Lakeland after his much heralded signing.

"He aired me right out. He told me he didn't care where the Tigers had drafted me. What I had done in college meant nothing to him. I was going to be on the field at 8 a.m. listening to what he said, and if I didn't, he said that he would send me home to my momma. I really believe he would have fought me.

"But, you know, he busted me, he challenged me, he demanded respect. He was instrumental in my making it to the bigs."

The scenario was repeated many times. But in 1979, with no advance warning, the Tigers hired Sparky Anderson, and the way to the Detroit dugout was blocked.

Leyland stayed in the organization another two years, and then began the journey as a coach and manager that would lead to three division titles with

The Detroit Tigers' Magical 2006 Season

Jim Leyland got out of managing in 1999 because he didn't have the energy to put out ego-related fires during his one and only season with the Colorado Rockies. Now, his passion is back. In 2006, he helped the Tigers get off to one of the most surprising starts in baseball history.

Jim Leyland happily awaits Curtis Granderson and Ramon Santiago after Granderson hit the game-winning single in a game against the Tampa Bay Devil Rays.

Pittsburgh and the Series victory with Florida.

He was so intense that he was once famously described as "a guy who makes coffee nervous."

Andy Van Slyke, who played for him with the Pirates and is now his first-base coach, put it another way. "I felt like a performance car with no fuel in my tank," he says. "Jim Leyland became my fuel. I feel like my career was more important to him than it was to me. I think a lot of managers say that, but the players will tell you that's not the case."

But the Tigers found out two other important things about Leyland in short order. He can accept winning or losing. But he will not tolerate sloppy preparation.

Many look back to the game of April 18 as a turning point of the 2006 season. The Tigers had broken away to an uncharacteristically good start and ended their first homestand of the year by splitting a four-game series with Cleveland.

But in the last game, before the start of a West Coast swing, the Indians had smeared the team, 10-2. Leyland was incensed. Not so much at the loss as by the fact he felt the team had simply given up and coasted through the last few innings.

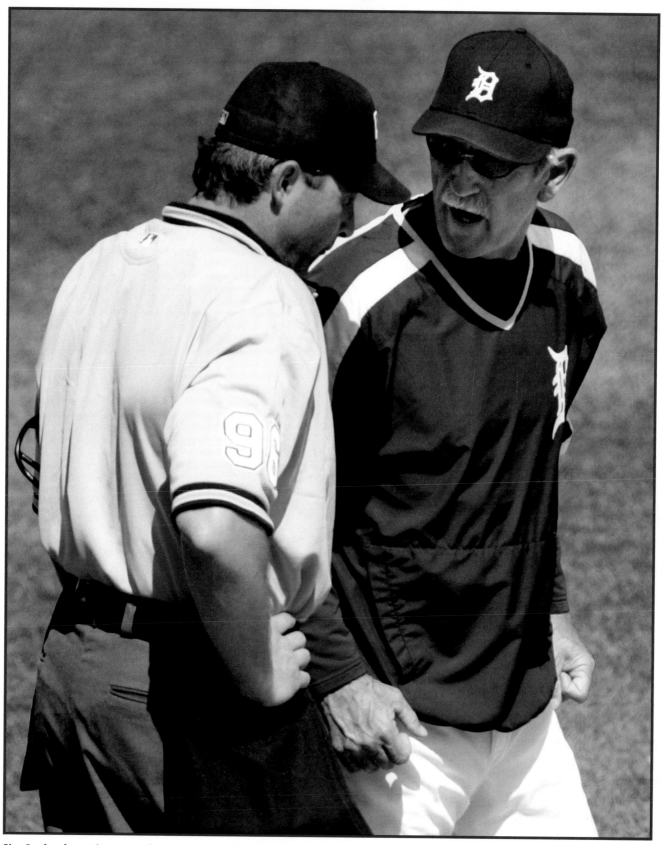

Jim Leyland continues to shout at home plate umpire Paul Nauert after being tossed in the eighth inning of a June game against the Boston Red Sox.

Jim Leyland smiles as he puts his arm around his son, Pat, in the dugout before a spring training baseball game between the Tigers and the Houston Astros in March.

He closed the clubhouse doors and lit into the Tigers. "This team will play the full nine innings," he said. "It will not give up on any ballgame."

The Tigers had never heard this kind of song before. The tone was set. From then on, the team had a different look about it.

Leyland also made it clear that he didn't go by the book. He would put on plays in unorthodox counts and situations. He would look at unusual match-ups, get everyone into the game as much as he could. He would personally visit a struggling pitcher instead of sending out his coach "to get negative thoughts out of his head."

He was forcing other managers to react to him instead of falling into the pattern of passive Tigers teams of recent years.

It also turned out that his claim about not knowing a thing about the Detroit roster was a big fib. He was perfectly aware of the strengths and weaknesses of his team. But he wanted to send a message that he hadn't made up his mind about anything. That would wait until he saw the effort on the field.

With the media, he was old school all the way; terse, direct answers that responded directly to questions without ever revealing too much. Cap pulled low over his brow shielding his eyes, he sat in the manager's office with his face a stoic mask.

Sometimes he would chide fans for treating each two-game losing streak as the start of the collapse. But who could blame them? Collapses were part of the game plan for so long.

But he also cautioned against untoward optimism. When asked if he felt secure with a 10-game lead, he responded that he would if there were nine games left in the season.

Sparky could get carried away and promise the moon and stars. But Leyland had his feet planted firmly on the ground.

He had waited too long to get them on this particular piece of turf. ■

The Detroit Tigers' Magical 2006 Season

Jim Leyland watches pensively from the dugout as the Tigers play the Cleveland Indians in the ninth inning. The Tigers won 4-1.

Big Red Sets the Tone
Shelton's Monster April Ignited the Flame

For two weeks in April, Chris Shelton was the biggest story in baseball. He hit nine home runs in his first 13 games, the quickest any player in American League history had reached that mark. He was the league's Player of the Week in the season's first seven days. On a bad day his batting average might drop below .500.

True, Detroit's record through those first 13 games was only 7-6. That looked terrific compared to some of the dreadful starts the team had endured in recent seasons. But the big redheaded first baseman had some of the old-timers talking about Norm Cash and his fantastic 1961 season, and many younger observers were stumped for any comparison at all.

Two homers on opening day in Kansas City and three hits the next game. Three more dingers along with two triples as the team took the next three in Texas. Two against Chicago at home and then two more against Cleveland.

To leftfield. To right. Against rookie pitchers and veterans. It didn't seem to make any difference. Anything that came to the plate ended up in the most distant recesses of the outfield.

It was Shelton's burst from the gate that first put Detroit fans on notice that this season would be a little different. It galvanized the city, even eclipsing for a while the start of the playoffs for the Red Wings and Pistons.

Those teams remained the big story. But it was nice to see the Tigers doing a little better, too.

"He's the real deal," said Leyland. "He's a good, young hitter who has the potential to be an outstanding old hitter. He'll have times when he struggles, but right now he's hitting pretty much everything."

The media, many of them from the national TV networks and publications, swarmed his locker. Shelton had become a one-man running story on ESPN. The Tigers? Oh, yeah. They were interesting, too, but Big Red, the nickname that was quickly hung upon him, was the headline.

He had come to the Tigers by the most innocuous of routes, as a Rule 5 draft pick, left unprotected by Pittsburgh. The Pirates had taken him out of the University of Utah and slotted him as a catcher. The problem was he wasn't a very good catcher, and not much better at first base. They began to wonder if, for all his skills as a hitter, there would be a position for him in the big leagues.

The Tigers, a team with nothing much to lose, decided to take a chance on a guy who had hit .334 in the minors the previous year.

"Our scouts thought he could hit at a big-league level because he swung a good bat and had a good command of the strike zone," said Dombrowski.

Under the Rule 5 provisions he had to stay with the team for 2004 and only got to bat 46 times. But as soon as he was sent down to Toledo in 2005, he was back into the .330s again. He was called back to Detroit May 31 and stayed the rest of the year. He finished one point below .300, and even with missing two

Chris Shelton is congratulated by teammates after his home run off Kansas City Royals starting pitcher Scott Elarton during the sixth inning of their opening day baseball game in Kansas City. It was the second home run of the game for Shelton.

OUT OF NOWHERE

Chris Shelton scores ahead of the tag by Houston Astros catcher Eric Munson. Shelton scored on a double by Brandon Inge.

months of the season had 18 homers and 59 RBIs.

But all that seemed merely a prelude after his blazing start in 2006. Bloggers were projecting 85 home runs---not seriously, of course. But Shelton looked to be one of the greatest natural hitters the Tigers had placed in their lineup in years.

He admitted that he had a chip on his shoulder about the Pirates turning him loose so cheaply. "All of my success is predicated on everybody telling me I can't do this or that," he said. "Maybe when the season is over, I can realize what I did to start the season and that I did something special."

When the Tigers played in Pittsburgh later in the summer, the newspapers there were climbing all over general manager Dave Littlefield for losing the sort of hitter their last-place team so badly needed. Just to punctuate it, Shelton slammed a home run that struck the wall behind the bleachers in dead center. It was one of the longest home runs ever charted in the Pirates' new ballpark.

In later years, Cash lamented that his .361 season in 1961 was "probably the worst thing that I ever did." Expectations were so high that he never could fulfill them again.

And in the sad words of Cole Porter, Shelton was also "too hot not to cool down."

Shelton himself noted even in the midst of his streak that he was striking out far too much. "I'm either hitting the ball out of the park, getting an extra base hit or striking out," he said on April 18.

The words were prophetic. By May the slow slide down the batting charts had begun. Pitchers were working him

Chris Shelton follows through in the sixth inning against Cleveland Indians pitcher Cliff Lee. Shelton hit his major league-leading eighth home run in the fourth inning, leading the Tigers to a 1-0 win over the Indians.

Chris Shelton smacks a three-RBI double off Minnesota Twins pitcher Kyle Lohse.

inside or getting him to climb the ladder and chase pitches high out of the strike zone. The strikeouts mounted and the raves of April turned into the rages of July.

Sports-radio callers vehemently insisted that Shelton's success had gone to his waist and that's why he couldn't handle the inside stuff. He still was hitting in the .270s, but his power production disappeared. After hitting 10 homers in April, only six more followed through July.

During his opening surge, Leyland batted him sixth. But he dropped him to seventh and when a tough right-hander was pitching he sometimes sat him down. If there had been a solid left-hand hitting alternative he probably would have sat more often. But Dmitri Young, who had been slated for that role, was battling personal problems and was away from the team until mid-July.

Finally, at the end of the month, the Tigers announced that they had acquired Sean Casey from Pittsburgh and Shelton was being sent to Toledo. Leyland emphasized he would be back by September 1 and that he still regarded him as "our first baseman of the future."

It was a shocking turnaround for a season that started so spectacularly. Still, if not for Shelton, the Tigers of 2006 would have lacked the opening kick that defined their April.

Whatever happened afterwards, Shelton had given them that…and it was quite a lot. ∎

Chris Shelton hits a single in the second inning against Los Angeles Angels pitcher Evan Santana.

A Gamble Pays Off

Rogers Acquisition an Instant Success

When Kenny Rogers was introduced at Comerica Park for the 2005 All Star Game, the boos came raining down from every part of the stands.

Just a few weeks before, the Texas Rangers left-hander had been involved in a tussle with a Fort Worth TV cameraman. He objected to a camera being stuck in his face as he came on the field, and endless replays of the incident made Rogers come off as a prize jerk.

Less than one year later, all the jeers had turned to adulation in Detroit when Rogers was picked to start the 2006 All Star Game. The 41-year old pitcher was the anchor of the most surprising pitching staff in baseball, the old head who gave guidance to the bevy of talented youngsters in the Detroit rotation.

He was first in the league to win 10 games, which also happened to be his 200th in the majors.

That June 19th game at Wrigley Field was another landmark of sorts. Thousands of Detroit fans made the trip to Chicago for the weekend series with the Cubs. Throughout the three-game sweep their cheers of "Let's go, Tigers," almost drowned out the hometown fans.

It had been a long, long time since Detroit fans had cared enough about the Tigers to go on the road with the team in numbers that were audible. But this year, they were ready to fill up their cars with $3-per-gallon gas and roll.

"When I heard it, I got chills," said outfielder Curtis Granderson, who was returning to his own hometown.

"The stars are lining up," said reliever Jason Grilli, who pitched the ninth in the easy 12-3 victory for Rogers. "It's a great thing to be part of something special."

"Everybody knows how I pitch by now," said Rogers. "The only question when I go out there is whether I have command of the strike zone. There are no surprises at this point in my career."

When asked exactly what it was that Rogers had contributed to the Tigers, all Leyland could say was, "There's so much I couldn't even begin to talk about it all. He brings a lot to the party."

The two other left-handed starters, Nate Robertson and Mike Maroth, were constantly at his side in the dugout, and he was also a settling influence on Justin Verlander in his rookie season.

"We talk about situations, approach, that sort of thing," said Verlander. "He's someone you listen to."

Quite a turnaround. After all, he was the same guy about whom the bloggers had said after he signed with Detroit, "the only mentoring he can do is in throwing tantrums."

The signing was indeed regarded as puzzling when the Tigers brought him in as a free agent the previous December. Maybe even worse than puzzling. This was how the Tigers were going to improve? By grabbing an over-the-hill starter?

Rogers was coming off his third go-round with Texas. He was known as a terrific fielder (he was a left-

The Detroit Tigers' Magical 2006 Season

Kenny Rogers lets one fly with passion against the Minnesota Twins. After the game, Rogers became the Majors' first seven-game winner this season and the Tigers extended their winning streak to a season-high seven games.

Kenny Rogers winds up against the Oakland Athletics. Rogers, who was named to the All-Star team in 2006, won his seventh straight decision against his former club in this game.

Kenny Rogers fires away in a game against the Kansas City Royals.

starter in a late-season double-header in 1918. He had been with the team as a coach.

Rogers turned in six innings in the Tigers' 3-1 win. That became his pattern. Keep the hitters off balance for two or three times through the lineup and then turn it over to the fireballers from the bullpen.

When he won Number 200 he was 10-3, and so respected by his younger teammates that they gave him a Number 200 jersey signed by all of them after the game.

Brandon Inge, who handled the presentation, said they expected him to be around for Number 300, too.

It was remarkable that he had even made it to 100. Rogers had two major arm surgeries before ever reaching the major leagues and was on the disabled list three years in a row. He spent seven long years in the deep minors—more than the length of the entire professional careers of most of the other pitchers with the 2006 Tigers—before getting his chance with Texas in 1989.

handed shortstop in high school) with one of the best pickoff moves in the game. He was also streaky, a guy capable of reeling off eight or nine wins in a row and then coming up empty for weeks at a time.

And then there was all that baggage of the shove seen 'round the world. He had never carried the reputation of being a hothead. But a few moments on television changes everything.

as his opening day starter in Kansas City. He had dealt with a lot edgier guys than him. Still, Rogers was the oldest pitcher to get that assignment in Tigers history. At the end of the day, he was the oldest to win any kind of game for the Tigers in 86 years; since Wild Bill Donovan had to go in as an emergency

There followed four years as a relief pitcher. So by the time he actually became a starter he was already 29 years old. That is ancient by starter standards, but he made the most of the time that was left to him. His has been picked for the All-Star team three times after reaching the age of 39.

By mid-summer, as Rogers went into a second-half funk, some Detroit commentators were urging that he be removed from the starting rotation.

But, like Chris Shelton, his contributions to the team's blazing beginning were incalculable. In the words of his manager, "He brought a lot to the table." ■

Kenny Rogers focuses after Chicago White Sox' Jermaine Dye's single during the first inning of a baseball game against their American League Central rivals.

Above the Radar
Rookie Flamethrower Zumaya Delivers the Heat

By the time the Tigers held their home opener, six games into the season, Joel Zumaya was already a folk hero.

Exactly 20 years and one day younger than Kenny Rogers, he could also be described as the anti-Rogers in pitching style. To paraphrase an old baseball axiom, he could throw the dawn past a rooster.

Only a few hard-core fans knew his name before the season began. He had flashed through the organization's two top minor-league teams in 2005, striking out 199 hitters in 151 innings at Erie and Toledo.

But that was as a starter. In his entire professional career, he had pitched relief just once and no one expected him to come north from spring training with the team. He was slated to get some more starting experience with the Mud Hens.

As Leyland watched him throw in Lakeland, however, he knew that he was not going to leave an arm like this in Toledo.

"An absolute stud," read one scouting report on Zumaya. "He throws a four-seam fastball at 96-100 miles an hour and a very nice hammer that he can drop at 82-84 miles an hour…which is absolutely lethal when you're throwing close to triple digits. His four-seamer is straight, but I still think it's unhittable."

The words were an accurate reflection of what Detroit fans saw after the season began. He had appeared only twice before the home opener, for a total of just four innings. But he gave up no hits and struck out three.

And when the TV camera focused on the section of the scoreboard that measured pitch speed, he was hitting the triple digits.

As he emerged from the bullpen for the first time at Comerica, a murmur began rising among the sellout crowd. It grew to an all-out roar as he reached the mound, a sound that would be heard many times through the summer to come. With his ruggedly handsome Latino looks, much of the cheering developed a distinctly high-pitched timbre.

Zumaya learned to feed off the sound, trotting in from the bullpen amid the commotion as if he could hardly wait to blow away whoever was standing there with a bat in his hands. Big strikeouts were punctuated with a wave of his fist and shout of triumph, a display that annoyed some opponents but delighted the fans.

This was the flame-thrower the Tigers had dreamed about. It was the role that Matt Anderson was supposed to have filled when he came to Detroit in 1998. But he could never master his control, and when he injured his arm in a Red Wings' sponsored octopus-throwing contest, of all things, his velocity never returned.

At his best, though, Anderson never reached the speeds Zumaya could attain.

Zumaya was just an oversized kid from the San Diego area. When he was growing up, his perfect day, he said, consisted of getting on a charter boat at 5 a.m. and spending the rest of the morning and afternoon looking for game fish out on the Pacific.

Reliever Joel Zumaya throwing heat against the Chicago White Sox in the eighth inning of a game. Zumaya recorded his fifth win as the Tigers beat the White Sox 2-1.

Joel Zumaya pitches to Philadelphia Phillies' Mike Lieberthal in the fifth inning of a spring training game. The young fireballer was already a folk hero by the Tigers' home opener.

Joel Zumaya pumps his fist after getting the side out in the eighth inning of a game against the Oakland Athletics.

His other favorite sport was soccer. To everyone's relief, he had absolutely no interest in hockey, or octupi.

"He tried to interest me in soccer during the 2006 World Cup," said Leyland. "But he'll be a manager before I'll be a soccer fan."

Zumaya's first home appearance was flawed when he gave up a home run to Chicago's Paul Konerko. But he really hit his stride on June 11th.

The Tigers were holding on to an 8-5 lead at Toronto in the deciding game of three at Rogers Centre. The Blue Jays were the best hitting team in baseball and they had cut into a Detroit lead, driving reliever Jason Grilli out with two men on base and

nobody out in the seventh. They had beaten the Tigers with an eight-run eighth inning two days before, and things were getting nervous.

When the call came in for him, Zumaya ruefully admitted, his attention had been diverted. He was watching the World Cup on a TV near the bullpen. "Next thing you know, I'm out there," he said.

And seven pitches later, Toronto was nowhere. Two pop ups and a strikeout of Lyle Overbay on three straight 99-mile an hour fastballs, and the threat was over.

Zumaya then sat down the Jays in the eighth and ninth, getting his first professional career save. "That was no freebie," said Leyland. The performance also convinced the manager that he could put in his rookie in any game situation. He still reserved the closer role, however, for the veteran Todd Jones.

The Toronto radar guns measured one fastball in the eighth inning at 102 miles an hour. Later in the season, some observers accused Detroit of juicing the guns at Comerica for psychological effect, making it seem that Zumaya was throwing even harder than he actually was. But that would not explain why the devices in Toronto would register the same speed.

Zumaya said early in the season that he was perfectly happy pitching relief and, in fact, was no longer interested in being a starter. But for a guy who won't even be 22 until a month after the season ends, there's still time to make that decision.

Life doesn't have to go at 102 miles an hour, too. ■

Joel Zumaya celebrates after getting the final out of the eighth inning in a Tigers' June game against the Boston Red Sox. Zumaya was averaging more than one strikeout per inning out of the bullpen and his fastball was clocked at a sizzling 102 miles per hour.

Blazing a Comeback Trail

Injury-free Ordonez Back to His Old Self

When ballplayers talk about a "professional hitter," Magglio Ordonez is the gold standard. Above all other skills the sport demands, his business is hitting a baseball hard and long. He has done it wherever he's played.

His colleagues admire the calm, analytical way he goes about his job; keeping his emotions in check, never getting too high or too low.

A good example of that came in the June 21 game at Milwaukee. Rick Helling started for the Brewers and took care of Detroit in the first inning on nine pitches, striking out the side. His tenth pitch was to Ordonez in the second, and it landed in the leftfield pavilion. The Tigers were off and away to a 10-1 rout. The rightfielder added a second homer later on.

To Ordonez it was quite simple.

"I saw that he was throwing all strikes to our first three hitters," he shrugged. "So I went up there looking for a strike and I got it."

"There's a reason he is who he is," said Helling afterwards. "It's not that he just hits me well. He hits everybody."

"You watch him after a game," said former Chicago teammate Paul Konerko, "and you can't tell if he went 4-for-4 or 0-for-4. That's just the way he is."

Watching him play in 2006 it would be hard to guess that the Tigers' cleanup hitter was coming off two of the most frustrating and tumultuous seasons of his career.

Inflammation and bone marrow edema in his left knee kept him on the disabled list for all but 52 games with the White Sox in 2004. It was the final year of his contract in Chicago, and as one of the most productive hitters in the American League, Ordonez could have expected to sign the most lucrative deal of his career.

Instead, he was perceived as damaged goods, a gamble, a severely limited performer who probably would not be worth the money it would take to sign him. The White Sox passed and so did everybody else.

He stayed available as a free agent until the eve of 2005 spring training. That's when the Tigers decided to take a chance and spring for a five-year, $75 million deal.

Then just three games into the season with his new team, Ordonez went down with a sports hernia and back on the disabled list. He didn't return until July 1, and when he did he was not the productive hitter the Tigers were counting on. He finished the season hitting .302 but it wasn't a strong .302, and every time he started to run hard management held its collective breath.

To make it even worse, the White Sox, the team with which he had spent all 14 previous years of his professional career, went on to win the World Series without him.

The frustration came bubbling out in an ill-advised interview while he was on the disabled list. He described Chicago manager Ozzie Guillen as "an enemy." He accused Guillen, a fellow Venezuelan, of forcing him to play on his bad knee and then discouraging the Sox from signing him.

"If he comes to me and wants to apologize, I still wouldn't accept it," said Ordonez.

Magglio Ordonez swings for the fences during a game against the Seattle Mariners. Ordonez was selected to play in the 2006 All-Star Game.

Magglio Ordonez reaches for home plate as Texas Rangers' catcher Rod Barajas stretches with both hands to make the tag. Ordonez was trying to score from second base on a single by Brandon Inge.

Magglio Ordonez looks for a sign during the first inning of a game against the Chicago White Sox.

Guillen, not known as the most temperate of individuals in the best of circumstances, went up in smoke, calling Ordonez "another Venezuelan bleep" and advising him to "shut the bleep up."

So when Ordonez arrived in Florida for the start of the 2006 season, he had a lot of things on his mind. Staying healthy, however, was no longer the primary concern. He'd spent the off-season at the University of Miami, working out with the Hurricanes football team in their training program. He was building up the strength that had produced 160 home runs and 590 RBIs in the five seasons before his injuries cut him down and robbed him of his power stroke.

"The last two years, I've been focused on my body," he explained. "It's hard to get ready for the game that way. Now I'm healthy."

"Everybody knew he's a great baseball player," said Brandon Inge. "But no one really knows how much the injury affected him. To do what he's done. He runs out every ball he hits. He's running down fly balls. He's tracking down everything."

One indication of the change was the flowing hair that curled down from beneath his batting helmet. He explained that his decision to go unshorn was part of his idea to approach the 2006 season as "something new." When he finally wanted to get it cut, he said, his wife wouldn't let him because she had grown to like it.

It's somewhat out of character for Ordonez, who grew up in a small village and favors a quiet, conservative demeanor. That's what made his outburst at Guillen so surprising. But it was an indication of what was seething beneath the deceptively calm exterior.

Jim Leyland, who knows a thing or two about intensity, appreciates Ordonez' perspective on the game.

"I don't need cheerleaders," he says. "I need hitters."

He led the team in RBIs most of the season, none bigger than the four he delivered in the June 1 game with the Yankees. The Tigers were on a four-game losing streak and in danger of getting swept at home in a four-game series with New York for the first time in 80 years. Then they fell behind in this one, 5-0.

But Ordonez started the comeback by drawing a bases-loaded walk in the fifth, added a two-run-single in the sixth and then set up the win with a game-tying single in the ninth.

It was a typical performance; not spectacular, but highly effective.

The best touch of the year came when Guillen, his adversary of the previous season, decided to patch things up and chose Ordonez as a reserve on the All Star team. "With the season he's having, he deserves it," he said.

A few weeks later he was nominated as the Comeback Player of 2006. And nothing more needed to be said by anyone. ∎

Magglio Ordonez connects on a run-scoring single against Minnesota Twins pitcher Jesse Crain in the seventh inning of a game. The Tigers won 9-3.

Straight Shooter
Fireballer Verlander Wise Beyond His Years

Of all the surprises that came from out of nowhere in 2006, the biggest may have been Justin Verlander.

Sure, he had been Detroit's top pick, and the second overall, in the 2004 draft. But the Tigers had made so many blunders in the draft that it was difficult to believe that they finally had done something right.

Yes, he'd had a rather spectacular 2005 in the minor leagues. Verlander went 11-2 with an overall earned run average of 1.29 at Lakeland and Erie. Those are impressive stats, but they were compiled at no higher than the AA level. Besides, it was only his first season of professional baseball.

Maybe he'd be ready in a year or two. But the leap from AA to the majors is forbiddingly wide.

The Tigers had taken him out of Virginia's Old Dominion University, and came close to losing him when the ballclub and Verlander's agent couldn't make a deal. It took an 11th hour intervention by his family to sign him.

When he flew up to Detroit, posed for the mandatory photo op on the mound at Comerica Park and spoke to team officials, the ballclub was impressed by his sincerity and work ethic.

What they already knew was that he consistently hit the upper 90s with his fastball. But it was his mastery of a biting curve, a changeup and control that really blew all the scouts away. The minors are filled with hard throwers who can't get it harnessed; guys who never get it through

their heads that major league-hitters will clobber 95 mile-an-hour fastballs if they don't show them anything else.

Verlander was a different breed of cat. By the end of 2005, he was ranked by baseball insiders as Detroit's top prospect and one of the best pitchers anywhere in the minors.

Still and all, who could have known that by the end of July he would be leading the American League with 14 wins?

Observers were reduced to carping about what they regarded as an "unacceptably low" strikeout ratio of only 5 per 9 innings. But one of the best games he pitched was his May 17 start against the Twins. Matched against former Cy Young Award winner Johan Santana, Verlander pitched eight innings of six-hit, shutout ball, and won the game when catcher Vance Wilson hit a two-run homer. What made his performance remarkable was that he neither walked nor struck out anyone, a stat line that rarely appears alongside a starter.

"That's usually not my style of pitching," he said. "They were aggressive on the fastballs. They were putting them in play, but not very solid. It worked well for me. I'll take no walks, no strikeouts, no runs anytime.

"I'm always going to be working on location, even if I have a 20-year career. Talk to me again in 15 years and I'll still be working on location. It's something that can always be better…it gives me something to work on every day."

He also credited the simple fact that he was in the big leagues and given the opportunity to learn from veter-

The Detroit Tigers' Magical 2006 Season

Justin Verlander throws against the Houston Astros in the eighth inning of a June game. Verlander pitched three-hit ball for eight innings in the Tigers' 5-0 win.

43

Justin Verlander throws in the fourth inning of a game against the Baltimore Orioles. Verlander threw for six innings and allowed seven hits in the Tigers' 6-3 win.

Justin Verlander pitches to Philadelphia Phillies' Shane Victorino in the first inning of a spring training game. Verlander was already showing signs of great promise as he pitched two innings and gave up no hits.

ans like Kenny Rogers with his rapid advancement.

"It may sound corny but I really do come in here every day, listening and talking to the veteran guys and seeing what I can absorb. As long as I can keep an open mind and keep learning, I think it will be good."

Verlander didn't even know it the first time his heater topped 100 miles an hour. He was still at Old Dominion and the university's radar gun only went to 99 miles an hour. He had to be told by some major league scouts, using their own hand-held detectors in the stands, that he had broken the triple-digit mark.

"I think it annoys him that he's not the fastest rookie in the league," laughs Todd Jones, "and not even on

his own team. [Joel] Zumaya can bring it harder than he can. But Justin says it's all apples and oranges, pitches from a starter and a reliever."

Still, two 100-mile-an-hour pitchers is a luxury not many teams enjoy. And Verlander says his mentality is still, "Here it is; try and hit it." High velocity is the primary weapon he relies on when he's behind in the count.

"I've never had a starter throwing 99 miles an hour in the eighth," says an impressed Leyland, before returning to his customary understatement mode. "With the equipment he has, I'd say he has a nice future."

But Kansas City's Doug Mientkiewicz was as shocked as Leyland when he saw it. "Not only was it 99 miles an hour but it was on the black," he told reporters. "That's as good a stuff as I've ever seen."

Minnesota's manager Ron Gardenhire was equally amazed, however, at Verlander's willingness to throw a curve or changeup no matter what the count was. "A 3-2 changeup?" he said. "That's pretty impressive for a young guy."

"He can throw all his pitches for strikes," says Nate Robertson. "No hitter I've ever talked to wants to face that."

Pitching coach Chuck Hernandez knew that Verlander had won a place in the rotation in spring training, although the rookie wasn't let in on that little secret right away. "He knows he can't just live off his arm and the stuff he had right now," Hernandez says. "He listens and wants to get better."

What pleases Verlander's friends and family most, however, is something a scout told them when Justin was still in college.

"Ten years from now," his father was advised, "the only difference between Justin then and Justin now is that he'll be driving a nicer car."

After he received a $3 million signing bonus with the Tigers, he put almost all the money into conservative investments. Then he and his longtime girlfriend went out and celebrated by playing computer games at a local arcade. ■

Flamethrowing phenom Justin Verlander follows through on a pitch to the Oakland Athletics in the second inning of a game.

Back in the Middle of Things

Sweet-swinging Guillen a Staple at Shortstop

It started with a triple in the second inning. The next time up he hit a home run, and then came the single.

When Carlos Guillen came to the plate again in the eighth, the outcome of the August 1 game was no longer in doubt. The Tigers were up on Tampa Bay by five runs and would go on to win 10-4.

So when Guillen sent a soft liner slightly into the gap in right center it appeared that it would be his fourth hit of the game and nothing more. But the Tigers shortstop had no intention of stopping at first. Before the startled Tampa outfielder could react he was steaming toward second and beat the throw for his cycle-completing double.

It was only the second time in the last half century that a Detroit player had accomplished the feat, and the first since Damion Easley did it in 2001.

"You've got to keep hustling no matter what the score is," Guillen said with a smile after the game. "That's what the manager keeps saying."

But there was little doubt that he knew exactly what he was doing, that it was a case of double-or-nothing in his final trip to the plate.

For Guillen it was an act of uncharacteristic glitter. Like his fellow Venezuelan, Magglio Ordonez, the shortstop prefers to keep it low-key and duck the spotlight, although he is regarded as a leader among the team's Hispanic players. Among the Tigers infielders he is also the most likely to approach the mound for a calming chat with the pitcher when things get a little rocky.

But the careers of Guillen and Ordonez have fol-lowed remarkably similar paths in Detroit.

One of the major reasons for Detroit's flop in 2005 was that Guillen, like Ordonez, was not himself phys-ically for most of the year. He'd undergone season-ending knee surgery late in 2004 and his mobility and leg strength still weren't fully restored when the new season came around.

He was in the lineup for little more than half the games and had to go on the disabled list twice. His range on defense was drastically reduced, and while he did hit a career best .320 it was an average with lit-tle vim in it. It was all very similar to Ordonez' season.

The two also had taken similar routes to reach Detroit. Guillen's former team, Seattle, looked at his history of injuries, his salary, an arbitration hearing coming up and his apparent lack of power. So the Mariners let him go to the Tigers in a trade for two minor-league infielders.

Of all the moves Dave Dombrowski pulled off as the team's general manager, this may have been the slickest. Guillen filled a huge hole in the Tigers defense, and also blossomed unexpectedly into a big-time hitter. His 20 home runs and 97 RBIs in 2004 were far and away the best numbers he ever put up. He ended the year hitting .318—also a new high—and was named to the All-Star team.

About his only high point in 2005, however, was getting into the middle of the team's biggest brawl of the year. He claimed a pitch from Kansas City's Rudelys Hernandez had hit him on the shoe, but after an argument with the plate umpire it was disal-

Carlos Guillen is congratulated in the dugout after scoring in the second inning of a game against the Oakland Athletics. Guillen scored on a base hit by Craig Monroe.

Carlos Guillen singles to right field in the first inning of a game against the Oakland Athletics. Guillen tripled, doubled and singled while leading starting pitcher Nate Robertson and the Tigers to an 8-4 victory.

Carlos Guillen looks toward first base after forcing out Joe Inglett in the eighth inning of a game against the Cleveland Indians.

lowed. Hernandez' next pitch hit Guillen in the helmet, touching off a wild, bench-clearing brawl that led to several suspensions.

As much as any of the rookie surprises or new acquisitions, it was the return to health of Guillen and Ordonez that were the most positive additions to the 2006 Tigers. They were both playing on two legs again.

Jim Leyland is old-school all the way, and may have been expected to look askance at Guillen deliberately trying for a personal milestone when he legged out his double in a game that already was well in hand. Not a bit of it.

"I think when you start singling guys out as being a little more special than somebody else, that's a mistake and I don't believe in that," says Leyland. "We need all 25 guys if we're going to compete. But is Carlos Guillen one of my favorites? Absolutely. He's more of a veteran guy that knows how to play the game.

"He's a professional player and a professional person. I think good things happen to good people, and he's good people. Besides, hitting for the cycle is a pretty special event."

His teammates had no problems with it, either.

"We were all lined up on the top step of the dugout when he came to bat," said Sean Casey, in his first week with the team. "I might have gone out there and tackled him if he hadn't tried for the double."

Oddly enough, the switch-hitter had just missed a cycle only nine days before, lacking only the home run in a game against Oakland. He also used three bats to pull it off. Guillen is notorious for borrowing his teammates' bats when he feels a need, and he uses different bats batting left-handed and right-handed.

Guillen had been involved in two walk-off hits in earlier games, including a homer in a 10-9 win over Kansas City in May and a single in a comeback, ninth-inning rally against the Yankees.

Winning teams don't always have a great shortstop. It makes things a bit more difficult but it can be done. The major case in point was the 1968 Tigers who rotated three players at the position during the season and finally had to call in Mickey Stanley from centerfield to play there during the World Series.

But when analysts talk about the necessity of strength "up the middle," it is usually a reliable shortstop who is the key. And if he can hit a little bit, too, that's gravy.

Alan Trammell was the paradigm for the Tigers, the best at that position in their history and the cornerstone of the 1984 World Champions.

Guillen may fall a little short of that exalted standard, and he chalked up a surprisingly large number of errors, mostly on throws, during the season. But it would be hard to imagine the 2006 Tigers would have contended without him. ■

Carlos Guillen drills a three-run home run during the first inning of a game against the Chicago Cubs in Wrigley Field.

The Graduate
Bonderman No Longer a Student-in-Training

Jeremy Bonderman has been with the Tigers for four seasons, so long a span by recent Detroit standards that he is considered one of the veterans. But he is just 119 days older than rookie Justin Verlander, and like the rookie star of 2006 Bonderman came to the Tigers with just one season of professional baseball under his belt.

So it's hard to remember sometimes that he is still just a kid. But Professor Jim Leyland had the answer to that situation. In the most widely quoted words of wisdom he delivered on the pitching mound this season, the manager told Bonderman that it was "time to graduate."

It happened in the May 24 game in Kansas City. While protecting a 5-0 lead in the sixth, Bonderman gave up a three-run homer to Matt Stairs, a player who always hit him well.

In the past, a setback like this would have caused the pitcher to lose focus and, in far too many instances, his game would vanish in a puff of smoke. But Leyland's Commencement Day speech seemed to turn his season, and maybe his career, around.

"I told him it's time to graduate and really become the major-league pitcher you can be," he said. "This is a perfect time for you to turn the page, get your concentration on the next hitter and put that [home run] in the memory bank somewhere. This is where you either graduate or you don't."

"You've got to step up," said Bonderman after that game. "You can't feel sorry for yourself."

Bonderman went on to earn his cap and gown. He shut out the Royals the rest of the way, and then embarked on the best streak of his career. In his next six starts his earned run average was 2.30. He allowed just 37 baserunners over that period while striking out 44. It's hard to pitch better than that. Only a lack of run support in several of those starts kept him from leading the team in wins.

Of course, it took more than Leyland's pep talk to get him going. It was right about at the same time that Bonderman began experimenting with a new grip for his changeup. It was a wrinkle taught to him by another senior member of the Tigers faculty, Kenny Rogers.

This was a pitch that had been ineffective for him throughout his career. Batters only had to watch for his fastball and slider. They were good, but with the change and a new outlook Bonderman became the dominating pitcher Detroit thought he would.

He came to the Tigers in one of the first big trades of the Dave Dombrowski regime. The team had finally concluded that Jeff Weaver was about as good as he was going to get. He shared many of Bonderman's attitude problems. A fluke hit, an error, and Weaver would go right up the chute. He also had the reputation as being something of a hothead.

But Weaver was regarded as the ace of staff in 2002 when Dombrowski dealt him to the Yankees in a three-way deal with Oakland. The Tigers wound up with first baseman Carlos Pena, relief pitcher Franklyn German, and a player to be named later, which turned out to be Bonderman.

The Detroit Tigers' Magical 2006 Season

Jeremy Bonderman is the leader of Detroit's young nucleus of pitchers that is as good as any team in the major leagues.

Not one to hold anything back, Jeremy Bonderman puts everything he has into a pitch against the Cleveland Indians.

Jeremy Bonderman is consoled by Ivan Rodriguez during a key moment in a game against the Cincinnati Reds.

It was a deal to which most Tigers fans responded with, "Huh? We gave up our best pitcher for this?"

Pena and German never panned out and were gone by the start of 2006. It was Bonderman who was the prize. In his one season of Class A ball, which was still in progress when the trade was made, he had a 9-8 record. But his strikeout ratio was high and his ERA acceptably low at 3.61. It was enough to make the Tigers very interested.

So in his second year as a professional, at the age of 20, he was dropped into the starting rotation of one of the worst teams in the history of baseball. Bonderman went 6-19, and the Tigers were slammed for that decision by many commentators. They argued he would have been better served while learning in the minors and that the mounting losses might break his spirit.

But his former college coach Geoff Zahn said at the time that Bonderman was ready for the challenge. His words turned out to be prophetic.

"Jeremy is 20 going on 30," said Zahn. "Athletically, he already has a major-league fastball and an outstanding major-league breaking ball. But where he stands out is in his mental maturity and toughness.

"He's learning in the toughest arena in the world. Jeremy told me, 'I want to win so bad; I am scared of failure. But they've told me that if I used that the right way it would help you, not hurt you.'"

"That is personal tutelage at its highest," said Zahn. "There is no way he could have gotten that education anywhere else."

Still, it's one thing to say it and another to make it happen. Bonderman showed steady improvement over the next two years, going 11-13 and 14-13. His stats also got better, if only marginally. He still fought himself in too many tough spots, and over the second half of 2005 he sagged to a 3-8 record. Still a pre-season report in *Sports Illustrated* named him as one of the possible "breakout pitchers" of 2006.

That was the situation when Leyland made his fateful trip to the mound in May.

Taking a pitcher one year out of high school and making him a big-league starter is one of the riskiest propositions in professional sports. There really is no parallel. While NBA stars with that experience step into a starting lineup frequently, it's a different game with different demands.

Sooner or later, however, school is out, and Bonderman has advanced to postgraduate studies, at last. ∎

Starting for the Tigers since the age of 20, Jeremy Bonderman has emerged as a potent force in Detroit's formidable starting rotation.

A Jewel at the Top
Leadoff Centerfielder Granderson a Real Gem

Centerfield at Comerica Park is a wide and lonesome place. Because of the dimensions of the playing surface, it is one of the most challenging outfield positions in baseball.

Added to that is the fact that Detroit's outfielders on the corners, Craig Monroe and Magglio Ordonez, are only average on defense.

The demands of this ballpark's centerfield have confounded the Tigers ever since they moved in. They sought avidly but never found the right player for the position. There were two candidates when the team arrived in Lakeland in 2006—Nook Logan and Curtis Granderson.

Logan had slightly more experience. He was a third-round draft pick in 2000, just as Granderson had been selected in the same round two years later. Logan also had sprinter's speed. He stole 219 bases in his minor-league career, and added 31 more when he played with Detroit in parts of two seasons. On a team as challenged in the baserunning department as the Tigers, that had to be a plus.

But there was something about Granderson that Leyland liked. Intelligence, the way he carried himself, the sort of assurance that didn't lapse into cockiness. He was ranked one of the top prospects to come out of the Chicago area in recent years and in his junior year at the University of Illinois-Chicago he had finished second in the country in batting among NCAA Division 1 schools.

"The kid's a jewel," said Leyland. "He works hard, and, more important, he works smart. You can see it on his face. He wants to learn. He doesn't have all the answers, but he wants to be a quality major-league player…and he's going to be."

Every jewel needs polishing, though, and Leyland had the right gemologist for that. He had assembled a coaching staff out of his old Pittsburgh cohorts. Among them was the great defensive centerfielder on his division-winning teams, Andy Van Slyke.

He was given the nominal assignment of coaching first base. But his most important job was working with Granderson.

"He's one of the reasons I love coming to the ballpark," said Van Slyke. "He's a terrific guy, he's got a good work ethic and he wants to get better. He has a desire to play the game right. Those are all the things you look for in a player."

As far as Granderson was concerned, the admiration was mutual.

"He has helped me in the outfield from the amount of work he forced me to do," he said. "The only way you're going to get better is to keep working at it. That's the mentality he has."

The lessons took. By the time the Tigers came north, Logan was in the rearview mirror and Granderson had the job. He went on to play the first 151 games of his big-league career without making an error, and that one was on a missed throw to the cutoff man. Tiger fans learned to expect that he would catch everything in play and

The Detroit Tigers' Magical 2006 Season

Curtis Granderson darts out of the batter's box on a go-ahead RBI-double to center field against the St. Louis Cardinals. Detroit's Alexis Gomez scored from first base and the Tigers went on to beat the Cardinals 4-1.

Curtis Granderson watches his
seventh inning home run sail
over the center field wall against
the Baltimore Orioles.

Curtis Granderson slides in safely beneath New York Yankees' shortstop Miguel Cairo as Cairo reaches for a wide toss from second baseman Robinson Cano in the sixth inning of a Tigers' 8-4 victory over the Yankees. Cairo couldn't reach Cano's relay on the play, allowing Granderson to reach base.

then do the right thing once he caught it.

If that wasn't enough of a burden for a rookie, though, Leyland also made Granderson his leadoff man. It was a bit of a reach. Granderson had not shown any particular ability to draw walks, a prerequisite for a leadoff hitter. He also was only an average threat to steal. But the Tigers didn't have a prototypical leadoff man on the roster and Granderson appeared to be the best by default.

"Later in his career he has enough power to bat somewhere in the middle of the lineup," said hitting coach Don Slaught, another of the old Pittsburgh gang. "But for now he'll do fine at the top."

By midseason Granderson was leading the team in walks.

His most memorable contribution, however, featured the long ball in one of many late-inning comebacks for the Tigers. Cincinnati had come into Comerica in late May and won the opener of a three-game weekend series.

In the Saturday night game, the Tigers let a big lead get away when Joel Zumaya came in and gave up a grand slam to Ken Griffey, Jr.

As it left the ballpark, Granderson was transported back to the house in which he'd grown up. His bedroom walls were plastered with posters of his hero, Griffey.

"I collected players' cards, too, and I was always looking for his rookie card," he said. "My mom would take me to garage sales all around our area so I could look for it, but I never found it. So for a split second after he hit that ball I was like, 'Wow, that was amazing there.' Then, all of a sudden it hit me that we were down and we had to fight back."

He also remembered that the guy who had given up the slam was his best friend on the club and roommate on the road.

It was still a 6-5 Cincy lead when Granderson came up with two outs in the ninth. On a 2-1 count he got a fastball and went the opposite way with it.

"I was thinking double all the way," he said later. "My whole goal right out of the box was to get to second or maybe third depending on what it did coming off the wall."

Instead, it cleared the leftfield wall by about three feet. The ball traveled around 100 feet less than Griffey's smash. But it tied the game and set up the Tigers' win in the 10th. It also came to typify a familiar pattern in 2006, a last-ditch big hit from an unlikely source.

"It may not come the first time through the lineup and it may not come the second time," said Granderson. "But everyone on this team has the mental attitude that they can deliver in the late innings. It's the way we play the game." ∎

The speedy Curtis Granderson scores another run against the Kansas City Royals.

The Man Behind 'Gum Time'
Southpaw Robertson Defines the Meaning of 'Persevere'

Sometime during the Tigers' late-spring surge, Nate Robertson was transformed from just another left-handed starting pitcher to Mr. Gum Time.

Televised images of Robertson in the Detroit dugout, stuffing his mouth full of all the Big League Chew bubble gum it could hold to spark a rally in the late innings, caught the fancy of the fans. Soon most of the other Tigers were chomping, too, until the entire bench looked like the survivors of a mumps outbreak.

Gum Time became the signature of this team; just as much as rally monkeys, caps turned inside out and terrible towels had worked for other teams and other sports.

Maybe it didn't have the ring of "Bless You, Boys," the rallying cry of 1984. But it was probably an improvement over "Go Get 'em, Tigers" from 1968.

From a guy who was tabbed at the start of the season as the No. 4 starter—and it was far from certain that he could hold on to that spot— Robertson had become an iconic figure; the living, chewing symbol of the Spirit of '06.

"They had me miked up for a home game with the Yankees in late May," Robertson explains. "So I thought I'd give the camera something good, and when we started rallying from behind I just popped all this gum in my mouth and started chewing.

"We didn't win that one but two days later we did come from behind to win it and I was chewing again. The TV guys loved it and signs starting showing up at the ballpark, saying things like 'Big Nate Chew.' "

Television play-by-play announcer Mario Impemba picked up on it and began referring to Gum Time as a regular feature of the late innings, while the camera panned across the busy jaws of the ballplayers.

"All the pitchers loved it because it gave us something different to do while we were on the bench cheering the guys on. But soon Carlos [Guillen] was stuffing his mouth, and when Sean Casey came over here he could hardly wait to join in."

ESPN began showing the pictures around the country as the Tigers became one of the summer's biggest stories. When the team showed up at their hotels in other cities their far-flung corps of fans greeted them with cheeks full of chew. And even though team officials are less than pleased when some used-up gum gets stuck to the bottom of seats at Comerica Park, the pastime has spread to the stands, too.

"We're having fun with it," says Robertson. "That's the biggest thing, keeping the innocence in the game. We used to do it in Little League, with gum or some pumpkin seeds. It's making everybody feel like kids again."

Robertson's carefree demeanor masks a bumpy road to success in the majors. Dave Dombrowski saw a lot of the promise and drafted him for the Marlins in 1999. After taking the Tigers job, he traded away one of his veteran starters, Mark Redman, four years later to bring Robertson to Detroit.

But the promise had remained just promise. He was only 7-16 in 2005, although much of that record was attributable to the fact that he received the third-lowest run support of any starter in the league.

Nate Robertson stretches at the apex of his pitch in the third inning of a game against the Texas Rangers.

Nate Robertson throws against the Chicago
White Sox in the first inning of a game.

Not afraid to show emotion on the mound, Nate Robertson reacts after getting the third out in a key moment.

When the new season began, fans buzzed about the promise of Jeremy Bonderman and Justin Verlander, and the well-honed skills of Kenny Rogers. In the minds of many observers, though, Robertson occupied the shakiest perch. The talk was he'd be out of the rotation by May.

Instead, he turned into one of the most consistent of the starters. He was getting right-handed hitters out with a nasty, darting slider and was fearless about attacking the strike zone and going after hitters with his hard stuff.

When the team plunged into a gut-grabbing, five-game losing streak in August, it was Robertson who pulled the Tigers out of it with a 7-4 win against Boston on the 14th. And that was in Fenway, known for decades as a left-hander's valley of doom.

Earlier in the season he had outdueled Roger Clemens, who was making one of his first starts of the year for Houston.

"His confidence level is up a lot," said Jim Leyland. "His maturity is up a lot. He's made tremendous progress."

Robertson, who has a deep respect for the game's history and lore, managed to grab the lineup card that night and placed it among his souvenirs. He had grown up in Wichita, Kansas and was an outstanding high school prospect. He was drafted twice by the White Sox, but turned down the money both times in favor of attending Wichita State University.

That decision looked a lot less advisable when he had to undergo major arm surgery while still in school on a torn flexor-pronator muscle mass. It's the sort of injury that has ended more than one pitcher's career.

He wrote the word "Persevere" under the bill of his baseball cap, went back out and compiled an 8-0 record for the Wheatshockers. He then spent most of his first two professional seasons on the disabled list before submitting to another operation, this time to his left elbow.

So it truly was an act of faith for Dombrowski to trade for him. And it also explains why Robertson puts the phrase "It's all about hope" at the top of his blog.

He now wears "Gum Time" tee shirts, but Robertson says the last thing he wants to do is commercialize the phenomenon. He gets e-mails from all across the country, almost all of them delighted with the fad and advising him that they have started chewing right along with him at home.

Maybe the real appeal of Gum Time touched something deeper among baseball fans. Because in the age of steroids there is a lot to be said for bubble gum as the magic ingredient for big-league success.

But the real story may be under his hat. Because the word "Persevere" is still what appears there. ■

Consistency has been a hallmark of Nate Robertson in the 2006 season.

More Hits Than Glitz
Polanco's Steady Hand Guides the Ship

If ever a ballplayer was perfectly named it is Placido Polanco. It describes exactly how he approaches the game; imperturbable, calm, quiet, placid.

Always making contact with the ball. Always making the plays at second base. One of the most reliable No. 2 hitters in the game, with a gift for making the hit and run click. Until a shoulder separation took him out of the lineup in August, he was the team's quietly indispensable man.

Polanco is not a guy who gets picked on fantasy teams. He doesn't hit many home runs. In fact, of all the Detroit regulars in 2006 he was the least likely to get an extra-base hit. He won't steal a lot of bases. Hitting in the second slot doesn't get him a lot of RBIs.

He just does the things that need to be done to win games. He is repeatedly described as a ballplayer's ballplayer. Or, to phrase it another way: "He is a manager's dream," says Jim Leyland.

"If you picture the hit he's going to get, it's a line drive over the second baseman's head," says hitting coach Don Slaught. "When you see that, you know he's right."

In a poll of players, only Cleveland's Travis Hafner was regarded as a better judge of the strike zone. Polanco led all players in 2005 in strikeout-to-at-bats ratio, fanning just once every 22 times. The other side of that coin is that he walks almost as rarely. He seldom even goes to a full count.

Usually, failing to draw walks is the mark of an undisciplined hitter. But Polanco succeeds in putting the ball in play somewhere on the field an incredible two out of every three times he swings the bat.

Taking all his statistics together he is probably the anti-leadoff man. Even so, Leyland does not hesitate to bat him there in games when a hard throwing left-hander is pitching against Detroit and Curtis Granderson gets the day off.

You will search the headlines in vain for reports of Polanco's spectacular game-winning hits. His contributions sometimes don't even make the box score. Hitting to the right side to advance a runner. Making the pivot and avoiding the baserunner to complete a double play. That sort of thing.

There were two exceptions to the quiet rule, though. Polanco was intimately involved in two of the biggest hits of the season. The first decided one of the Tigers' most significant extra-inning thrillers. The other big hit caught him squarely in the face.

The hit off his bat came on June 25, in the middle game of the team's sweep of St. Louis. Marcus Thames was the big news of the night with a game-tying home run in the ninth. But that still left the game up for grabs.

In the tenth, the Cards' left-handed reliever Tyler Johnson made the mistake of walking Granderson. He had accomplished the rare feat of striking out Polanco the night before, however, so Tony LaRussa left him in to face him again. Johnson fell behind on a 3-1 count, knowing a walk would put the winning run on second.

"He struck me out on a breaking ball and I didn't

The Detroit Tigers' Magical 2006 Season

Manager Jim Leyland congratulates Placido Polanco after Polanco hit a double in the 10th inning to beat the St. Louis Cardinals 7-6. Polanco's double drove in Curtis Granderson from first base.

Placido Polanco exults on his way to first base after hitting an RBI single against the Oakland Athletics

Jumping over Tampa Bay Devil Rays' Aubrey Huff after getting the force out at second, Placido Polanco fires to first base for a double play.

that you can stand up after taking the hit, it doesn't seem so bad," said Polanco. "It wasn't until I saw the tape next day that I got scared. It looked worse there than it did when it was happening.

"I even wanted to stay in the game and for sure I wanted to play the next day. But the jaw had swelled up pretty bad, so I sat for a few."

The Tigers gulped hard at a disaster narrowly averted.

Close to being a .300 career hitter, Polanco is another member of the team who came to Detroit through Dave Dombrowski's astute appraisal of another ballclub's needs.

Polanco had been a solid performer with the Phillies. But they had Chase Utley coming up through their system and he was rightly regarded as a rising superstar. So Polanco became the expendable man in the summer of 2005. Philadelphia was willing to let him go, and shed his veterans' salary, for the paltry price of a utility infielder and a relief pitcher.

After coming to the Tigers he hit .338 and finished with the second highest overall batting average in the majors for the season. Unfortunately, the deal took a macabre turn during the winter when the former Detroit pitcher involved, Ugueth Urbina, was arrested in his native Venezuela on a charge of murder.

Polanco actually made up for one of Dombrowski's rare missteps with the Tigers. He had signed Fernando Vina as a free agent before the 2004 season to be the regular second baseman. But Vina went down with a leg injury barely one month into the season and never played for the Tigers again.

Polanco was brought in to set things right. As it turned out, things were rarely righter at the position.

Come to think of it, the two greatest second basemen in the team's history—Charlie Gehringer and Lou Whitaker—were also known as guys who didn't have a lot of glitz in their game. Maybe it comes with the territory. ■

want to see that again, so I worked the count a little," said Polanco, who seemed almost apologetic about taking three balls. "I saw the fastball and got the good part of the bat on it."

It was a typical Polanco double, into the right-center gap and deep enough to score the speedy Granderson.

The other hit came about a month later and was a lot scarier. In a game with Oakland, Polanco was trying to lay down a first-inning bunt against Esteban Loaiza. The pitch came in high and tight and caught him flush on the jaw. Aside from losing Mike Maroth, the Tigers had managed to stay clear of injuries up until then. But this looked like a bad one.

"You get caught up in the game and when you realize

Placido Polanco drives in a run with a single off Oakland Athletics' pitcher Joe Blanton.

Back in the Swing
Closer Jones Finds Old Magic upon Return

In the realm of Detroit sports, there are three positions that don't have much of a comfort zone: goalie for the Red Wings, quarterback for the Lions, and closer for the Tigers.

Play at one of those spots and you are almost guaranteed massive critical abuse and the job stability of a used-car salesman. Todd Jones took it once. The remarkable thing is that he came back in 2006 to take it again.

After three blown saves in early June, the sports-talk show hounds were baying for his blood. They said that Jones was the closer only because Jim Leyland kept calling him the closer. They said that the Tigers absolutely had to make a desperation trade with Atlanta to re-acquire John Smoltz after 19 years and install him as the closer in return for Joel Zumaya.

The deal existed only in the minds of the hysterical. But it was a measure of the early lack of confidence in the team's staying power that much of the fan base was ready to raise the white flag on Jones at the first sign of trouble.

But, in all fairness, even the manager was having his doubts. When Jones gave up a ninth inning, two-out, two-run homer to Kevin Youkilis in a tough 3-2 loss to Boston, Leyland made no secret of his displeasure. What bothered him was that Jones and catcher Vance Wilson had conferred on the mound with a one-strike count on the preceding hitter, Mike Lowell, who then singled.

"I don't have a problem when a guy makes a pitch and a guy hits a home run," said Leyland. "What I have a problem with is when you get two quick outs and you have strike one, you don't call the catcher out to talk about something. That's the kiss of death."

"That's what happens who you give up a home run with two outs in the inning," said Jones. "You open yourself up. That's the way it goes."

Been there. Blown that. Let's move on.

Jones has been called a living Maalox Moment. Ernie Harwell used to call him the Roller Coaster in his earlier stint with the Tigers. What really matters, though, was that after these late-spring eruptions, Jones went on to close out every lead he was called on to protect for the rest of June, July, and into August.

In one situation, in fact, he and Leyland conspired to psych out an opposing hitter familiar with Jones' earlier problems. With a two-out, two-strike count, Leyland came racing out of the dugout, as if to go over an unexpected variation in Jones' usual pitching pattern.

Instead, the two men said nothing and Jones came in with a fastball across the plate. This was the last thing the hitter expected and he froze. The called third strike ended the game.

"I don't like to make excuses because all it comes down to is having the ability to block everything out and make pitches," says Jones, in explaining his mindset. "I just have to try to stick and move, stick and move, because I don't have that knockout punch. You just have to keep making better pitches."

For several seasons, it seemed that Jones had lost any punch he may once have possessed.

The Detroit Tigers' Magical 2006 Season

Reading signs from his catcher, Todd Jones concentrates on the mound in the ninth inning of a game against the Boston Red Sox.

Todd Jones is congratulated by catcher Vance Wilson after the Tigers beat the Cleveland Indians 4-1 in a late July game.

During spring training, Todd Jones, who was about to turn 38, was in a position where he had to prove to the Tigers that he still had something left in the tank.

He had been Detroit's closer for parts of five seasons, from 1997 to 2001, and did a pretty good job for some pretty bad teams. He ended up saving 142 games before moving on to Minnesota.

In fact, his entrance into ballgames was one of the early crowd-pleasers when Comerica Park first opened. The home bullpen was then in right field. (It moved to left when the fences were shortened in right). Jones would come striding out of the pen and slam the gate behind him with emphatic force. The symbolic reference to closing the door always drew cheers.

But in the next four years he wandered among five different clubs. He was even cut by the hapless Tampa Bay Devil Rays one year in spring training. He was seldom used as a closer, his earned run average climbed, and, at 37 years old, it appeared that the ride was just about over for him.

Then he found a place with Florida in 2005 and it all came back. He saved 40 games, and for the second part of the season was almost unhittable. He converted 12 straight opportunities in August, a Marlins record for a single month.

Not bad. But when the Tigers picked him up as a free agent just before Christmas of 2005 it seemed to their fans as if they had found a lump of coal under the tree. Most closers are notoriously up-and-down, and Jones had been through many more downs than ups in recent seasons. He hadn't even especially wanted to sign with the Tigers. His first choice was Atlanta, because the Braves were always contenders and were not far from his year-round home in Alabama. But the Tigers offered him a two-year deal and that swung the balance.

For their part, the commentators said that if he and Kenny Rogers were the best the team could do in the free-agent market, the Tigers were in pretty sad shape. Which shows how much the commentators know.

Jones is one of the more astute students of the game. During the season he writes a weekly column for a Detroit paper. He also is fully aware that he had the honor of throwing the last pitch at Tiger Stadium in 1999.

He was so taken by that moment he even slept in the clubhouse the night before so he could more fully absorb all the history around him. He then sat enthralled as the greatest Tigers of the past were called onto the field after that final game to be introduced.

Most of them had played on pennant-winning teams. That was something else for Jones to think about as the 2006 season rolled along. ∎

Vance Wilson celebrates a 6-0 win over the Minnesota Twins with Todd Jones. Wilson hit a three-run double in the sixth inning to help lead the Tigers to victory.

Opportunity Knocks
Hard-Nosed Thames Makes the Most of an Overdue Chance

It was just a hard slide, nothing malicious. Old-school baseball, the kind that breaks up heads and double plays.

When Marcus Thames laid out Chicago second baseman Tadahito Iguchi to keep an inning alive, and Chris Shelton followed with a double that won the game, it was regarded as the signal that the Tigers were no longer anybody's pushovers. And Thames was happy to be the messenger.

"The throw from third base hung him out to dry," he said. "I didn't want to hurt the guy but I wanted to let him know I was coming. When I got up and heard the crowd going crazy, I knew something good had happened."

"It was the difference in the ballgame," said Jim Leyland. "I don't see it as playing hard. That's just baseball, but that's good baseball. The White Sox play it that way, too."

Even Ozzie Guillen agreed with that assessment, even though his player had been overmatched by about 40 pounds.

"I don't care. That's the way to play the game," he said. "I think when you do that, you show intensity. I was applauding."

Guillen recalled that when he was a rookie shortstop with Chicago, Kirk Gibson had taken him out with a slide just like that. "The next day he came in at me again and I threw the ball right at his head," he said. "Gibson loved it."

Thames's July 20 episode gave Detroit the odd game in a series at Comerica Park with the White Sox breathing down their necks. The image of Iguchi flying through the air after getting walloped became one of the symbols of the season.

For Thames, regarded as a player with limited resources whose only contribution to the party was the occasional long ball, it was part of a breakthrough season. During much of the summer, even though he was not in the lineup regularly, he led the team in home runs and played a credible leftfield.

There are many theories about when Alan Trammell lost control of his ballclub during the 2005 season. But there are those who say it happened right at the end of spring training, when the club made the decision to send Thames back to Toledo and keep Bobby Higginson on the Tigers roster. Thames had been a terror during the exhibition season, hitting for power and leading the team in RBIs. It was taken as a matter of course that he would go north with the team.

Higginson, on the other hand, was obviously near the end of the line. But he had been with the team since 1995, the longest service with the Tigers by far, and had actually played with Trammell. He was also in the last year of a very lucrative contract.

No one would say where the ultimate decision was made or why or by whom. But it was duly noted and it made players suspect that old strands of loyalty may have counted for more than performance.

Higginson, as it turned out, went on the disabled list early in 2005 and hardly played at all. Thames was

Marcus Thames rounds third base to greetings from coach Gene Lamont after Thames hit a two-run homer off Pittsburgh Pirates' starting pitcher Kip Wells.

Marcus Thames belts a solo dinger in the fifth inning of a game against the Cleveland Indians.

Marcus Thames hits a two-run home run to tie the baseball game against the St. Louis Cardinals at 6-6 in the ninth inning Saturday, June 24, 2006, in Detroit. The Tigers beat the Cardinals, 7-6, in 10 innings.

soon recalled from Toledo, but he never seemed to regain the traction of spring. He hit only .196 for the Tigers, while racking up his second straight .300 season in Toledo.

Leyland decided early on that he would keep an open mind about Thames. He was encouraged in this regard by input from his brother. Leyland grew up in the Toledo area, and many members of his family still live there. His brother, Larry, is a Mud Hens fan, and he told the manager that Thames only needed the opportunity to hit in the majors.

The move paid dividends on the night of June 25,

when Thames delivered one of the more dramatic ninth-inning blasts of the year. The two-run shot tied the game against St. Louis, and the Tigers went on to win it in the 10th.

"I have a request for [Tigers owner] Mr. Ilitch," Leyland laughed afterwards. "I want to put my brother on the payroll.

"There's no magic to this. We grind it out. We come to work and it's our responsibility to play nine innings, or, in this case, ten. That's what we're paid for. We don't get paid for four or five innings."

Thames had been working on an 0-for-4 night when he caught hold of Jason Isringhausen's cutter and launched it 410 feet. "I just saw it coming into my zone," he said. "It was a rough night until then."

But an admiring Curtis Granderson says that's just the thing about Thames. "Every time he's up there, he always looks like he's going to do something special," he said. "He has that look where the guy on the mound better be careful…with every ball that comes to the plate."

Thames had once been regarded as a top prospect with the Yankees. But playing in that organization is a tough way to go. The road ahead is frequently blocked by free-agent acquisitions. After parts of seven seasons in the minors, the Yankees, flush with experienced out-fielders, dealt him to Texas. But his one trial with the Rangers was brief and uneventful and the Tigers were able to draft him as a minor-league free agent before the 2004 season.

"All he ever needed was an opportunity," said Craig Monroe, his best friend on the Tigers. Ironically, he got that opportunity when Monroe got his leg tangled in some outfield padding and was reduced to designated-hitting duties for a couple of weeks.

That's when Thames had the chance to bust loose, hitting 17 home runs in his first 200 times at bat. That's what he was supposed to be doing all along. But the knock-'em-down-style slides expanded his arsenal. ∎

The Detroit Tigers' Magical 2006 Season

Marcus Thames celebrates after scoring the tying run against the New York Yankees in the bottom of the ninth inning. The Tigers beat the Yankees 7-6 when Ivan Rodriguez scored from second base on a single by Carlos Guillen.

Mr. Clutch
Monroe Makes Transformation When the Game is On the Line

For a player to be known as "clutch" is the most admired designation in baseball. In a game in which the fear of failure is always present, the clutch ballplayer succeeds in driving it out of his mind when the game is on the line. It is a rare gift and it is sometimes bestowed on those whose statistics may be otherwise average.

Tommy Henrich, for example, was overshadowed by many stars on the great Yankees teams of the late 1930s and 40s. But he was the one man his teammates wanted up there in the ninth, and they called him "Old Reliable."

So it is with Craig Monroe.

Somehow along the way, this lifetime .270 hitter becomes the most feared man in the Detroit lineup when things get late and tight. He can come to bat three times in the game and look absolutely awful. But on the fourth time around something electric takes place and he becomes a dominating force.

"He has shown to himself and to everybody else that when it gets late in the game he pays a whole lot of attention and he gives you a quality at-bat every time," says Todd Jones. "That's all we can ask for."

Monroe has some trouble explaining it himself.

"You try to do the things that you know you've worked on," is all he says.

Hitting coach Don Slaught believes it is Monroe's newly found ability to foul off good pitches and extend the at-bat that gives him the opening to deliver.

"He's got an air of confidence about him now that he knows he can do it," says Jim Leyland. "I think the biggest factor is that Craig Monroe wants to be up there in that situation. There's no doubt about it. He wants to be up there now."

And he is not discouraged when things go slightly awry.

In the August 3 game at Tampa Bay, for example, he just missed a ninth-inning shot that would have put the Tigers ahead. It landed barely foul and the team ended up losing. The very next night, he came up in the same situation at home against Cleveland, and once again the ball hooked just foul.

You could almost feel the ballpark sag. "All I could think of was 'Man, not again,' " said Jones.

On the next pitch, Monroe put it out for the home run that won the game, 7-6.

"Balls are going to go foul," he said. "Then there's going to be that one where you stay way inside of it and it stays fair. Hitting that ball foul almost gives you confidence. You tell yourself, 'I've seen his fastball and I fouled it off. I've seen his slider and I almost hit it out. What else has he got?'

"So now you relax a little bit because he doesn't have anything else to show me. He threw a fastball. My timing was good, my swing was good. We win."

It's that simple.

The only other players who matched Monroe's 2006 stats for late-inning big hits were David Ortiz and Albert Pujols.

Some of his late heroics are a bit more memorable

Craig Monroe hits a two-run home run off Cleveland Indians' pitcher Fernando Cabrera in the eighth inning. The Tigers won 7-6.

Craig Monroe beats the ball to home plate as Milwaukee Brewers' catcher Chad Moeller waits for the throw. Monroe sped home from second on a hit by Nate Robertson.

Craig Monroe is greeted by teammate Marcus Thames after Monroe hit a solo home run in the seventh inning of a game against the Seattle Mariners.

than others. He delivered a spectacular July grand slam, for example, against the White Sox. Chicago had routed the Tigers, 7-1, in the series opener. The game disturbed Leyland because he said that his team did not compete.

The next night they were being blanked into the sixth, 2-0, by Javier Vasquez. Then Detroit began sending a bunch of bouncers and bleeders through the Chicago infield. When Monroe came up, the bases were loaded, there was one out, and the score was 2-1.

He was in an 0-for-10 slump and a sacrifice fly would have been nice. Instead, he put it all the way out. The scoring was over for the day and the Tigers had a 5-2 win. They also won the next day, and defended their home turf against their closest pursuers. But the comeback began with Monroe.

"They'd been flipping me curveballs and sliders all week," he said. "I think the scouting report said, 'Throw Craig a slider. He ain't gonna' hit it.'

"But I feel if I make contact, good things are going to happen. I can hit a ball pretty hard. That was by far the biggest one I ever hit, though. The atmosphere, the team we were playing. You can't even describe it."

Sometimes he delivers in little ways, too. In the August 15 game at Boston, with the game tied 2-2 in the ninth, he sent a slicing looper down the right-field line. It couldn't have traveled more than 200 feet. Wily Mo Pena got a glove on it, couldn't hold it and the Tigers scored the winning run.

Monroe and his closest friend on the team, Marcus Thames, followed remarkably similar paths to Detroit. The two men, born eight days apart in 1977, had kicked around in the minors for years. Both had brief and unsuccessful stays with the Texas Rangers and ended up as free-agent draft picks from that organization by the Tigers, less than two years apart.

Monroe preceded Thames as the slugging leftfielder in the Toledo lineup and made it up to the big club to stay, once again, two years ahead of Thames.

The fact that they both play the same position and could be considered rivals hasn't diminished their friendship. They are each other's biggest fan.

"He knows where I'm coming from," says Thames. "When I'm not playing he goes up to watch my film and lets me know what I'm doing wrong. I do the same for him. We just try to be there for each other and keep each other going, keep each other positive. Because we both know how hard it is."

"It is hard when you don't get the opportunity to play," says Monroe. "But Marcus now has a manager who believes in him and that makes all the difference in the world. It's fun to watch."

But Monroe in the clutch is the most fun of all. ∎

Curtis Granderson celebrates with teammates Ramon Santiago, Zach Miner and Craig Monroe after hitting a single to drive in Brandon Inge and beat the Tampa Bay Devil Rays in the 13th inning of a dramatic game.

Meet the Mayor
Late Acquisition Casey Fits Into the Puzzle

The most significant clue, said Sherlock Holmes, was the dog that failed to bark. The expected thing that did not occur was just as important as anything that did.

So it was with the Tigers in 2006 and their trade-deadline acquisition of Sean Casey.

All through July, it was assumed that Detroit would have to make a deal for either Bobby Abreu of Philadelphia or Alfonso Soriano of Washington. The Tigers needed one more bat, preferably swung from the left side, to solidify the roster for the playoff run. Craig Monroe would probably be the price, and maybe a lot more, too.

As it turned out, the most significant development was the deal that was not made for a player who was not even on the Detroit roster. All Dave Dombrowski kept hearing in his discussions was one name—Cameron Maybin. And that was enough to shut them down.

The Tigers finally had some players in their system that other teams coveted. Maybin headed the list. He was the top draft pick in 2005, and while still playing at the Class A level the outfielder is rated the best prospect in their system. They were not going to mortgage the future. It had taken too long to build.

Besides, they were haunted by the memory of 1987 and the deal which brought Doyle Alexander from Atlanta. The price then had also been a minor leaguer, John Smoltz. Alexander pitched Detroit into the playoffs but quickly departed, and the Tigers have not been back since. The loss of Smoltz has stung for 19 years. It

wouldn't happen with Maybin. That dog won't bark.

But a lifetime .300 hitter who makes all the plays at first base and also swings from the left side was not a bad consolation prize. Casey was hardly mentioned at all in the trade rumors, possibly because he had spent much of the season on the disabled list with back problems.

The price Pittsburgh wanted was a minor-league pitcher and for the Tigers to take Casey's big salary off their hands. The deal was made and everyone pronounced themselves pleased with it; most of all Casey, who described himself as "ecstatic."

"How can you not be upbeat? I couldn't ask for a better situation," he said. "The word came through on the same day I was closing on a new house in Pittsburgh. I thought that was going to be the biggest thing that happened to me that day. But I'm not complaining."

Casey could hardly wait to get on a plane to Tampa and join his new team.

"My wife didn't mind me leaving so quickly because she knows what this means to me," he said. "I spent eight years in Cincinnati and we never made the playoffs. We sure weren't going to get there with the Pirates this year. So to come to this team is unbelievable for me.

"Look, I know they got where they are without me. For me to expect to hit third or fifth like I did for most of my career is unrealistic. I'll hit wherever they plug me in and give them whatever I can."

The contributions came quickly. He hit a home run in the first series he played at Tampa. Then with desperation staring the Tigers in the face after a three-game

Sean Casey bangs a two-run double against the Cleveland Indians in the seventh inning of a game. The Tigers beat the Indians 7-6.

The consummate contact hitter,
Sean Casey hits one to the
opposite field in a game
against the Minnesota Twins.

Sean Casey settled in quickly at first base for the Tigers upon his timely arrival late in the season.

sweep by Chicago, Casey contributed big hits that helped them win two straight in Boston: A two-run single off the left-field wall and a hit-and-run single to right.

It was the nature of the hits as well as the timing that was important. He uses the whole field and can handle the bat like a slap hitter. On a team noted for the impatience of its hitters, Casey also knows how to shrink the strike zone. Over his career he has walked

just about as much as he's struck out, while his slugging percentage is around .460.

He hit over .300 in five of his seasons with the Reds. But when his power numbers seemed to be fading, Cincy let him go to Pittsburgh after the 2005 season for a relief pitcher.

"I played with him in Cincinnati and I know what he's about," said Dmitri Young. "He just will be good for this team."

That is another consideration in making a late trade. The element of team chemistry can be overstated, but when it goes bad it can turn poisonous in the clubhouse very fast. A team has to be careful about the personality of a new player it brings into the mix.

The Tigers of '68 had added Eddie Mathews during the previous season's unsuccessful pennant run and he immediately played a leadership role. In '84, it was Ruppert Jones. Casey was the man for '06, and the fact that his nickname was "The Mayor" was a reassuring sign.

"Everybody likes him," says Vance Wilson. "He enjoys talking to everyone. He's just good to be around."

Almost overlooked in the delight over his bat, was what he brought to the party with his glove. It is significant that just before the trade was made, the former starter at first base, Chris Shelton, made two critical errors in a series with Minnesota. Young, who took over briefly at the position, then committed three errors in one game, including two dropped throws.

Casey drops nothing, and while he is one of the slowest runners in the league he can get into the hole on the right side with a quick first step.

Playing for Leyland also fulfills a childhood dream. He grew up in Pittsburgh, rooting for the Pirates teams he managed in the early 90s.

"There is no doubt that he's happy," says Leyland. "I told him when he got there that I just hope after seeing him play for a while that I'm happy.

"But he fits right in. He's a gamer and he likes to win."

And another piece in the puzzle clicked securely into place. ■

Sean Casey follows his hit down the first-base line in a game against the Minnesota Twins.

The Uber-Athlete
Inge Makes Adjustments to Find His Role

The NBA likes to bill itself as having "the world's greatest athletes." Major League Baseball cannot really make the same claim.

It has a bunch of guys with great hand-eye coordination. They can mash a baseball 450 feet or throw it 100 miles an hour.

Some ballplayers have the speed of a sprinter and some perform with the fervor of the football players they once were. But mostly they possess highly specialized skills, peculiar to baseball alone.

And then there's Brandon Inge, who can do just about anything. Or so the rest of the Tigers believe.

In a summary of his athletic achievements compiled by the *Detroit Free Press*, Inge can drive a golf ball 360 yards, dunk a basketball (at a listed height of 5-11), throw a left-handed curveball from behind his head, and once kicked a 50-yard field goal at Ford Field.

"I can't even explain it," says Curtis Granderson.

Inge was a shortstop in college. So, logically enough, the Detroit organization turned him into a catcher, a position he had never played before. It did not go so well. In parts of three seasons with the Tigers, his batting average was .194. On the other hand, the opposition stole a lot of bases on him.

Then things got a lot worse. Before the 2004 season began, the team signed Pudge Rodriguez. There was no doubt about the catcher now, and it sure wasn't going to be Inge. So by sheer doggedness and athletic ability he turned himself into one of the best defensive third basemen in the game.

"I don't know anyone who throws it better than Inge," says Jim Leyland.

But his arm is almost the least of it. Some of his plays—diving down the line to take away a double, charging in for the one-handed scoop on a dribbler, ranging to his left into the gap—are, in the words of Joel Zumaya, "freakish…pretty ridiculous stuff."

Catchers who move to other positions are usually adequate fielders, at best. Most of them end up as first basemen. Very few become spectacular at the other infield stations.

To veteran observers, Inge most closely resembles Mickey Stanley; an outstanding centerfielder who was placed at shortstop for the 1968 World Series after a total preparation of six games at that demanding position. No one on that team, however, doubted that he could do it. And so it is with Inge.

"If he had stayed at catcher he would have become a helluva catcher," says Leyland. "He just had too much to learn in a short time to think about hitting."

But maybe some of that focus carried over. Besides his athleticism, Inge is also developing a reputation as a thinking-man's ballplayer.

Typical was the game with Cleveland on August 5. With the Tigers down a run in the ninth, Inge batted leadoff and bunted to get on base with a single. Most players in that situation would have been trying to jack one out to get the tie. But Inge, who has home-run power, approached it another way.

"I'd noticed that the corner infielders had been play-

Brandon Inge strokes an RBI-single in a game against the Kansas City Royals.

Brandon Inge crushes a three-run home run in the seventh inning of a game against the Baltimore Orioles.

The smooth-swinging Brandon Inge swings away against the Tampa Bay Devil Rays.

ing me deep all game," he said. "So I went to Jim before coming to bat and talked it over with him. I'm trying to get something going at that point. If I hit a home run, that ties it, that's great. But if they're going to give it to you, I'm going to take it.

"Plus, closers don't like being bunted on. It's that whole power mentality."

So Inge pushed one to the right side of the mound, barely off the pitcher's glove. Two outs later, it was Rodriguez who delivered the home run that won the game.

"I never heard it that loud in this ballpark before," said Inge. "Not ever."

He ought to know. Inge is the only player still on the big-league roster who was there when Dave Dombrowski arrived in 2001. His tenure with the Detroit organization goes back to 1998, easily the longest on the team.

"You can't appreciate this season as much as the guys who were here for the bad times," he says. "For us, this really is kind of gratifying."

Inge was also a key participant in one of the strangest records the team set during the summer. On July 25, the Tigers became the first big-league team in 115 years, since the St. Louis Browns of the American Association in 1891, to score five or more runs in the first inning three games in a row.

Detroit did it twice against Oakland in a weekend series at Comerica Park (and ended up splitting those games, to Leyland's dismay) and then did it a third time in Cleveland. The hit that tied the record was a three-run, opposite-field blast by Inge.

"Sometimes when you score that many that early, it seems like you just sit back and not like you're fighting or giving max effort," he said. "Of course, we are. But still, the feel of the game is that you're kind of sitting on a lead and whatever happens happens. On the flip side, a five-run lead is a five-run lead."

Leyland's thinking was more or less along the same lines.

"I don't think it's impressive," he said. "What I think it is, is weird."

"If we can score five runs in the first inning every night, we're gonna have one helluva year," said the more pragmatic Todd Jones.

Inge feels he is still mastering the intricacies of playing third. The toughest adjustment was in coming from a position that was involved on every pitch to one where the action comes fast and unannounced.

He also knows that he sometimes gets impatient as a hitter and his strikeout-to-walk ratio is too high.

"He's still got to make adjustments at the plate," says Leyland. "Hell, they all do."

But having ridden to the bottom with the Tigers, Inge is relishing the chance to make the adjustments to life at the top. ■

The Detroit Tigers' Magical 2006 Season

Also a solid defensive player, Brandon Inge fields a ball from Cincinnati Reds' batter Edwin Encarnacion during a game. Encarnacion was thrown out at first base.

A Leader Reborn
Rodriguez Recaptures the Spark that First Brought Him Here

If you had to pinpoint a date at which the fortunes of the Tigers began to reverse themselves it would almost certainly be February 4, 2004. That was the day on which Pudge Rodriguez decided to sign with Detroit.

Everyone immediately understood that this was the most significant free-agent acquisition in the history of the franchise. Not so easy to understand was why.

Why did a sure Hall of Fame catcher decide to marry his fortunes to the worst team in baseball? He was coming off a World Championship with Florida in 2003. What was he doing scrounging around in baseball's dank basement?

Sure, there had been some concern that time had taken its toll on his 32-year old body. Catchers take a terrific beating and age faster than other position players. But still...the arm, the .300 lifetime batting average, the ability to handle pitchers. This was genuine greatness.

Alan Trammell attended the signing press conference with the look of a man who had been staring down at the gutter and found the winning lottery ticket.

"You'll have to excuse me if I just sit back and soak this up a little," said the manager.

"I know things have been bad here but I think they are going to get better," said Rodriguez. That was a safe bet. It is impossible to decline from 43-119. Privately, Pudge told people, "I know the Central Division and I can own it."

The $40 million, four-year was deal was hedged with safeguards for the Tigers about his physical condition. But he responded with one of his best years; a .334 average, another All-Star selection, 85 RBIs and a team leader in every sense of the word.

But that was then. In 2005, the team did not improve. He reported to Lakeland looking as if he had been on the Atkins Diet times two, with rumors of steroid use swirling around him after publication of former team-mate Jose Canseco's tell-all book.

He was going through a nasty divorce. His batting average fell over by 60 points. He didn't like the trade of his old buddy, Ugueth Urbina, to Philadelphia, even though it brought in an outstanding second baseman in Placido Polanco. He also felt that a trade-deadline deal that sent reliever Kyle Farnsworth to Atlanta was an indication that the team had given up on the season and was not serious about building a contender.

He was described as a cancer in the clubhouse. Probably more than any single individual it was Pudge who sabotaged Trammell's control of the team. The thinking was that no matter who the new manager was, Rodriguez would be traded for whatever the Tigers could get.

Now flash ahead a few months.

"I'll do anything Jim Leyland wants," he says. "He's the boss, he's the manager. I do what he tells me to do. I'm an everyday player and I'm going to go out there and do my best. It doesn't matter if I hit third, first, sixth, ninth, tenth, eleventh...whatever. It doesn't matter, man. He has an idea and we have to respect that

The Detroit Tigers' Magical 2006 Season

Ivan Rodriguez waits for a pitch during a game against the Seattle Mariners. Pudge was selected to play in the 2006 All-Star Game.

Ivan Rodriguez is held back by teammate
Carlos Guillen as Rodriguez yells at
home plate umpire Tim Timmons after
disagreeing with a questionable call.

A more serene Ivan Rodriguez smiles during a break in the action of a game against the Seattle Mariners.

idea. It's what is best for the team. For me, it's not a problem at all."

On one memorable occasion, the night that Polanco was hurt and the team was left without another infielder, Rodriguez went out and played second base. For the first time ever. He even ranged into short right-field to pull down a pop fly.

The scowl was gone. Now he was a cheerleader, the jolliest dude in town.

When he smacked a two-out, two-run, walkoff homer against Cleveland on August 5, he reacted like a kid—waving his arms as he dropped the bat and leaping into the welcoming popcorn machine at home plate. He was having as much fun as the 22-year old rookies.

Winning can do that. But, apparently, Leyland had something to do with it, too.

It didn't take a genius to know that among his top priorities was keeping Pudge happy. From the first lineup card he made out, Rodriguez was batting third. He stayed there…right up to the moment when it no longer made sense to bat him third against tough right-handed pitchers. Not with Dmitri Young swinging from the left side. By that time, however, it was not an issue anymore.

"This is my 16th year in the big leagues," said Rodriguez, "and I always play this game like it was my first. I love this game. Last year I didn't have that. This year, I have it.

"It was tough, but there's some way you take those things in a positive way. You can learn. It was a tough year but the important thing is I did my best. But it's already over and it's time to move forward."

Leyland insisted that all he ever told Rodriguez was just to be himself.

"If Pudge is patient he's going to hit," said the manager. "If Pudge is swinging at the first pitch, nobody's going to hit. He's always been good using the strike zone. He got away from it and he paid for it. It doesn't take a rocket scientist."

With that foundation in place, Rodriguez bought into the system, and when the time came to shake up the batting order he was on board. Of such things are great managers made.

But just as important as his hitting was the way he handled and steadied Detroit's young pitchers. In tandem with Kenny Rogers and Justin Verlander, two pitchers with outstanding pickoff moves, it also became nearly impossible to run on the Tigers. Opponents learned that trying to steal their way into scoring position was not a good tactic, which relieved an enormous amount of pressure from the pitching staff.

"Pudge wears his emotions on his sleeve," says Leyland. "Some guys will go back to the dugout after striking out and slam down their helmets or kick something. They do it every time and you start to ignore it because it gets to be phony. With Pudge it has an effect. He cares so much. The other guys have to care, too." ■

Ivan Rodriguez watches his two-run double in the third inning of a Tigers' 10-4 win over the Houston Astros.

Purging the Demons
Young Gets Self, Stroke Straightened Out

It could have been a great night for Dmitri Young. In the sixth, he had launched an enormous home run into the right-field pavilion for Detroit's only run against Texas.

When Craig Monroe led off the ninth with a triple, he came up with the chance to tie the game. He worked deep into the count before sending a hard shot right at the first baseman for the out.

As it turned out, the Tigers failed to score and lost the game. But Young had been through too much to complain. Any night he was back in the Detroit lineup was a great night for him.

"When you love something and almost have it taken away," he said afterwards, "you tend to hold on to it tight—metaphorically speaking."

In this season of gain for the Tigers, Young almost lost it all. In May he was arrested for allegedly beating up a woman friend at a suburban hotel. He then fell out of sight until turning up at a clinic in California to be treated for drug and alcohol addiction.

It was a shocking fall for a man who had always been among the friendliest and most approachable of the Tigers. Watching him play ball and interacting with his teammates, you'd swear that Young was a man without a problem in the world.

If the inner demons were there, he had kept them well-hidden.

One of Dave Dombrowski's first acts with the Tigers was approving the deal that brought the switch-hitting slugger to Detroit from Cincinnati. He had hit wherever he played and batted over .300 in four straight seasons with the Reds.

But it was difficult finding a position for him and Cincy was after more speed. In the American League, Young would be the perfect designated hitter, and in a pinch could fill in at first, third, or left-field for a short time.

In 2003, during the Tigers' sickening plunge into the abyss, Young was a rare point of light on the roster. With almost no protection around him in the batting order, he managed to hit .297, drive in 85 runs, and hit a career-high 29 home runs.

It was an amazing performance, about the only thing Tigers fans had to cheer about. His numbers tailed off somewhat in the following two seasons. Still, he was just 32 years old and tagged for DH duties again. More than that, he swung a dependable left-handed bat in a lineup overweighed with right-handers.

And then he wasn't there anymore.

On July 22, he returned. It was two months to the day that the Tigers had placed him on the disabled list to work out his problems. Young said that he had come back with a companion—"my conscience." He had been clean and sober for 60 days.

Behind the smiling face, he said, was an angry man. Bitter over a divorce and separation from his three children.

"Dealing with that, going down that road," he said, "you have a tendency to put yourself out there in the wrong situation. That's what I did."

Dmitri Young slices a single against Red Sox' pitcher Josh Beckett in the first inning of a game at Boston's Fenway Park.

Dmitri Young punches a double off
Houston Astros' pitching ace Roy Oswalt.

Dmitri Young peers out of the dugout during a game against the Philadelphia Phillies.

Problems with substance abuse have become an all too familiar part of contemporary athletics. In earlier years, bad drunks were often treated as lovable eccentrics, part of the game's color. Their careers and health destroyed, they faded from sight and were forgotten until the brief obit appeared on the wire services.

But when multi-million dollar contracts are at stake and with new cultural attitudes about substance abuse, there is nothing lovable about it anymore.

The Tigers welcomed Young back to the clubhouse. They wished him well as a human being. But they were also in a pennant race and everybody in Detroit knew that the Tigers badly needed some left-handed power to balance their lineup. If Young couldn't provide that, the game would go on without him.

He had been massively ineffective during the first part of the season. When he left the team he was hitting .169 with no homers and 4 RBIs. He looked overmatched even by mediocre pitching.

Which Dmitri would be coming back? Would it be the former slugger or the feeble shadow of the spring?

"I'm accepting him back as a person, as a teammate, anything," said Brandon Inge. "I don't know where the perception came from that we disliked him. As a friend, I'm glad to have him back. But production…that's the bottom line. We're a baseball team. That's what we're paid for."

Jim Leyland, as always, knew the score.

"I'm here to win games," he said. "We have to find out if Dmitri Young can hit. How we go about that is a problem. But if he can hit, that's a good problem."

Young seemed to answer the question immediately with two hits and two RBIs in his first game back against Oakland before a cheering Comerica Park crowd. He went on to hit 5 home runs in his first 8 games.

The question that everyone in the organization was asking had been answered. How desperate was Detroit's need to obtain a solid left-handed bat? Would it be worth trading prospects to get it? Young's return made it clear that the DH situation was solved, and that a measured trade for Sean Casey could be made without giving away too much. That was no small contribution.

By mid-August, Leyland had elevated Young to the number three slot in the batting order against right-handed pitchers. But Young's satisfaction went far beyond those concerns.

In a press conference before his first game back, he said "this is more than baseball. It's something I have to deal with for the rest of my life. I need to be a great father, a great friend--the stand-up person I always wanted to be."

In the classic baseball musical Damn Yankees, the lyric to one song goes: "A man doesn't know what he has until he loses it."

Mark it down as one of the eternal verities, in baseball as in life. ∎

Dmitri Young gets a fourth inning base hit during a spring training game against the Los Angeles Dodgers.

The Supporting Cast

Real Champions are Defined by Their Role Players

Every successful baseball team must have role players; those who also serve by knowing and accepting a place that fills one specific need.

It is in the use of these players that managers make a difference. Mayo Smith used to say that the moves a manager makes during a game are pretty much dictated by circumstances. "It's the 25 guys," he said. "That's what managing is."

Sparky Anderson felt that in knowing the capabilities of his entire roster, he would be able to put each player in a place "where he has a chance to succeed."

Think Tom Matchick and Rusty Kuntz, Daryl Patterson and Marty Castillo. Not the guys of prime-time memories, but those who made the most of their moments in the sun.

The Tigers of 2006 had their share:

Zach Miner:

While other Tigers rookies had their names and reputations precede them to Detroit, this guy arrived in almost perfect anonymity. He wasn't even on the 40-man roster during spring training. No one considered him a top prospect. He had been a throw-in the previous July in the deal that sent Kyle Farnsworth to Atlanta. The man the Tigers wanted was Roman Colon, and Miner just hitched a ride.

But when Mike Maroth went down with arm problems in May, this was the guy the Tigers brought up to replace him in the rotation.

"I had no idea what to expect from him," said Jim Leyland. "I knew almost nothing about him."

Miner came through with six straight wins, including a stalwart three-game run against Houston, Pittsburgh and Seattle in June. Leyland was careful to get him out at the first sign of trouble and he had fairly generous run support. But he was able to pick up for the absent Maroth for the best part of three months and preserve the cohesiveness of the starting rotation.

Jamie Walker:

Almost by definition, Walker has been the quintessential role player in Detroit. His job is quite simple. He comes out of the pen in the late innings, usually with runners in scoring position, to get a big left-handed hitter.

That's it. On many occasions, it's the only man he'll face. He's been doing it for four years, so he's kind of used to it by now. He's done it so well, that only Brandon Inge and Dmitri Young have been on the roster longer than he has.

With the Tigers bullpen better stocked than it has been in recent memory, his string of leading the club in appearances was broken at four straight years. On the other hand, his control, which had always been good, became phenomenal. In his first 41 innings he walked only five—and two of those were intentional.

Fairly typical of his performance was the August 6 game with Cleveland. He was called into a 1-0 game to face Travis Hafner, one of the most dangerous clutch hitters in the game, with the bases loaded.

Zach Miner throws a pitch during the ninth inning of a game against the Milwaukee Brewers. Miner pitched a complete game as the Tigers won 10-1.

Jamie Walker pitches against the Kansas City Royals in the eighth inning of a game in July. Walker replaced starter Justin Verlander in the eighth inning and the two combined for a three-hitter in the Tigers' 6-0 win.

Vance Wilson congratulates closing pitcher Todd Jones after the Tigers beat the Boston Red Sox 3-2 in an August game in Boston. Jones got the save, his 33rd of the season.

Hafner would go on to tie a record with six grand slams in one year. Walker struck him out.

Vance Wilson:

This is the other side of the equation. Hafner's strikeout occurred in a day game following a night game, when Leyland chooses to rest Pudge Rodriguez. So Wilson was the man behind the plate working with Walker.

That was a bit of a problem in 2005. Wilson got off to a slow start and finished the season hitting only .197. No one questioned his catching skills. But when he was acquired from the Mets the Tigers thought they were also getting someone who could fill in for Pudge with just a slight step down in offense. In 2006, the hitter they thought they had returned. Wilson was hitting close to .300 for a good part of the summer.

But like many backup catchers he was also a keen observer of the game. That's why so many of

Vance Wilson rounds the bases on a two-run home run during the fourth inning of a game against the Chicago Cubs. The Tigers won the game 12-3.

OUT OF NOWHERE

Zach Miner bears down during a game against the Oakland Athletics.

Fernando Rodney:

Sometimes it just takes one pitcher to make the entire bullpen fall into place. The Tigers had been waiting for Rodney to become that man for eight years.

He had been on the disabled list six times—once for chicken pox and the rest for various strains to both arms and shoulders. But he had shown enough in the minors to make up for two ineffective turns with the Tigers.

In 2005, he seemed to turn a corner. He spent most of the season in Detroit, had a 2.86 ERA and saved nine games. But things would be different in 2006. The previous year, the Tigers were trying to close games by committee. There was no one designated for the role by Alan Trammell.

With Todd Jones coming back to town, though, that job was spoken for under Jim Leyland. Rodney's value would be as the second set-up man. Ideally, Joel Zumaya would come in around the seventh, blow people away, and Rodney would pick up the pieces in the eighth to prepare the way for Jones. A mental change was required, far more than a mere change in mechanics, the problem that had bothered him earlier in his career. Leyland understood and gave him all the support he could.

In June, he said that "if I had to pick just one of my guys for the All-Star team it would be Rodney. What he has done is outstanding."

A little later, when things had soured a bit with some rough outings, Leyland was still in his corner.

"I've been through a lot," Rodney said. "I'm better now. Every time I go out and have a good situation or a bad situation, he tells me, 'Nice job. I know who you are. You know you're not perfect. Sometimes you're going to have a bad day.'

"That makes me keep working, keep my head up. Never get down."

The end result is an end-of-game bullpen that is among the strongest in baseball. ■

them—-Leyland, Mike Scioscia, Ralph Houk—-make good managers.

"In the grand scheme of baseball, Hafner's weaknesses will always be his weaknesses," says Wilson. "That being said I knew that his weakness was chasing pitches outside after the pitcher established a fastball inside."

For his part, Walker trusted Wilson implicitly.

"He's seen what Hafner's doing the whole game and I'm just watching from the bullpen," says Walker. "So when he says, 'This is how we'll start him off,' this is where our relationship has to work.

Role players in action can be a beautiful thing to watch.

Fernando Rodney pitches against the Boston Red Sox in the ninth inning of a game. Rodney relieved starter Jeremy Bonderman during the eighth inning and held the Red Sox hitless, striking out two and walking just one batter. The Tigers beat the Red Sox 6-2.

The Detroit Tigers' Magical 2006 Season

The heart, soul, and leader of the Detroit Tigers, Ivan Rodriguez, celebrates scoring the winning run on a Carlos Guillen hit off New York Yankees' pitcher Kyle Farnsworth.